Forest of Eyes

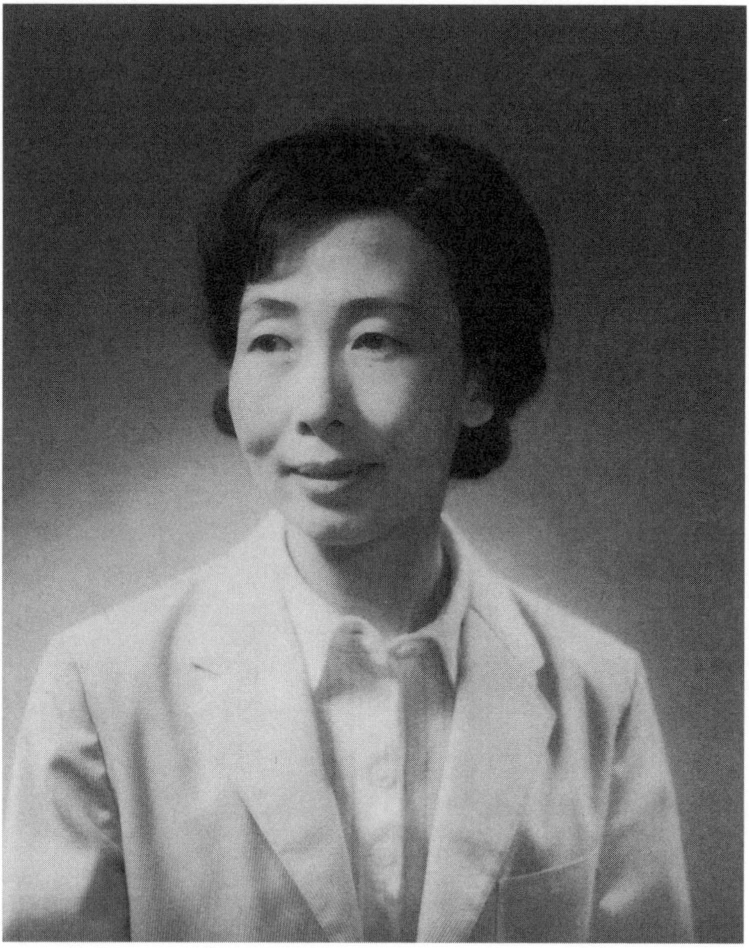

Forest of Eyes

Selected Poems of Tada Chimako

Translated from the Japanese and with
an Introduction and Notes by Jeffrey Angles

University of California Press   Berkeley   Los Angeles   London

University of California Press, one of the most distinguished university presses in the United States, enriches lives around the world by advancing scholarship in the humanities, social sciences, and natural sciences. Its activities are supported by the UC Press Foundation and by philanthropic contributions from individuals and institutions. For more information, visit www.ucpress.edu.

University of California Press
Berkeley and Los Angeles, California

University of California Press, Ltd.
London, England

Frontispiece: Tada Chimako ca. 1960–1965. Courtesy Suzuki Maya.

© 2010 by The Regents of the University of California

For acknowledgments of previous publication, see credits, page 155.

LIBRARY OF CONGRESS CATALOGING-IN-PUBLICATION DATA
Tada, Chimako.
[Poems. Selections]
   Forest of eyes / selected poems of Tada Chimako ; translated from the Japanese and with an introduction and notes by Jeffrey Angles.
      p. cm.
"The publisher gratefully acknowledges the generous support of the Joan Palevsky Literature in Translation Endowment Fund of the University of California Press Foundation."
   Includes bibliographical references and index.
   ISBN 978-0-520-26050-4 (cloth : alk. paper)
   ISBN 978-0-520-26051-1 (pbk. : alk. paper)
   1. Japanese poetry—Translations into English. 2. Japanese poetry—Women authors—History and criticism. 3. Women and literature—Japan. 4. Surrealism—Poetry. 5. Haiku—Translations into English. I. Angles, Jeffrey, 1971–. II. Title.
   PL862.A3A2 2010
   895.6'15—dc22
                                                  2010001664

Manufactured in the United States of America

19 18 17 16 15 14 13 12 11 10
10 9 8 7 6 5 4 3 2 1

The paper used in this publication meets the minimum requirements of ANSI/NISO Z 39.48-1992 (R 1997) (Permanence of Paper).

The publisher gratefully acknowledges the generous contributions to this book provided by the following organizations:

JAPANFOUNDATION

The Suntory Foundation

The Joan Palevsky Literature in Translation Endowment Fund of the University of California Press Foundation

This book was selected as the winner of the 2009 Japan–U.S. Friendship Commission Prize for the Translation of Japanese Literature. The prize was established in 1979 and is administered by the Donald Keene Center of Japanese Culture at Columbia University. It is the oldest prize for Japanese literary translation in the United States. Works entered into competition are judged on the literary merit of the translation and the accuracy with which it reflects the spirit of the Japanese original.

Contents

ix *Translator's Acknowledgments*
xi *Note on the Translation*
1   *Introduction*

13 FROM Fireworks (1956)
20 FROM The Gladiator's Arena (1960)
27 FROM Universe of the Rose (1964)
31 FROM The Town of Mirrors, or Forest of Eyes (1968)
38 FROM A False Record of Ages (1971)
51 FROM The Four-Faced Path (1975)
60 FROM A Spray of Water: *Tanka* (1975)
66 FROM Lotophagi (1980)
76 FROM Ceremonial Fire (1986)
91 FROM Along the Riverbank (1998)
106 FROM The Land of the Long River (2000)
110 FROM A Souvenir of Wind: *Haiku* (2003)
114 FROM Upon Breaking the Seal (2004)
121 FROM Person of the Playful Star: *Tanka* (2005)

135	*Translator's Notes*
147	*Chronology*
151	*Selected Works*
155	*Credits*
157	*Index of Titles and First Lines*

Translator's Acknowledgments

Although she is no longer here to see this book of translations, the utmost thanks must go to Tada Chimako herself. In 1998, when I first visited her home at the base of Mt. Rokkō, the graceful mountain that stands over the city of Kobe, I found Tada to be a perfect embodiment of the gentle erudition and subtle humor that fill her work. We spent an afternoon chatting over tea and homemade apple cake, discussing mythology, world literature, her memories of Marguerite Yourcenar, whose work she had translated, and her friendship with the poet Takahashi Mutsuo, whose work I had translated. Later, she guided me through her garden, pointing out the enormous eucalyptus tree near her house that had inspired the prose poem "Yūkari no ha o kaminagara" ["Chewing on a Eucalyptus Leaf"] and sharing with me the breathtaking view of the deep ravine that appeared in many of the poems in *Kawa no hotori ni* [*Along the Riverbank*]. The gardenias were blooming that day, and as I left, she picked a perfect flower and handed it to me in a spontaneous act of elegance. When I visited her garden again in 2005, over a year after her death, I once again found the gardenias blooming. In 2009, when I visited her family in the same home, there was a single gardenia blooming, two months out of season, as if Tada were sending me a gift from another world.

In 2002, a year after her diagnosis of cancer, I wrote to Tada and proposed translating this volume of her poetry. Because she was in hospice at the time, she responded via her daughter, Suzuki Maya. Even after Tada's death, Suzuki, a young psychologist who exhibits the same learned sophistication as her mother, has been thoroughly supportive of this project. I thank both Tada and Suzuki for their permission to translate these works as well as their comments regarding the translations. It is my great regret that Tada did not live long enough to see the publication of this collection.

I am also indebted to the poet Takahashi Mutsuo, who first introduced me to Tada Chimako's poetry and arranged for me to meet her. I thank the many people who have shaped the way that I read Japanese poetry and Tada's work in particular, including Suzuki Sadami and Alexa Foresster, as well as the helpful anonymous readers for University of California Press. I extend my warmest thanks to Dick Davis for all he taught me about translation, as well as to my colleagues in the Department of Foreign Languages at Western Michigan University, especially Cynthia Running-Johnson, Peter Blickle, Rand Johnson, Peter Krawutschke, David Kutzko, Mustafa Mughazy, Dasha Nisula, and Rika Saitō, who continue to believe strongly in the value of literary translation even when many academic institutions consistently fail to recognize its vital importance. I also thank my fellow faculty members in the Soga Japan Center, especially Steve Covell, Priscilla Lambert, and Takashi Yoshida.

Earlier versions of some of the translations in this collection have appeared in various journals and books. I thank the following editors for their encouragement and their permission to reprint the poems included in their collections: Anna Bernhard, *Tricycle;* Alan Botsford Saitoh, *Poetry Kanto;* Tina Chang, *Language for a New Century: Contemporary Poetry from the Middle East, Asia, and Beyond;* Jennifer Kronovet and Stefania Heim, *Circumference;* Sawako Nakayasu, *Factorial;* Olivia Sears, *Two Lines;* and the editorial staff of *Buddhadharma.* The editorial wisdom and sharp eyes of Rachel Berchten at University of California Press and of Jan Spauschus have made this book better in many small but significant ways. I thank them for believing in this project.

Without the kind encouragement and constructive criticism of Hiroaki Sato and Kyoko Selden, this project would not have been possible. Professor Selden was especially helpful in providing a thorough reading of the manuscript and suggesting many small but important changes. This book owes a profound debt of gratitude to both of them. I will always be grateful to the judges who granted this book the 2009 Japan–U.S. Friendship Commission Prize for the Translation of Japanese Literature. The prize helps to bring valuable recognition to translators, and it gave me a great boost of encouragement at a moment when I truly needed it.

These translations are dedicated to the late William J. Tyler, for all the guidance and friendship he provided over the years. He was both a true scholar and a great translator—a role model who shaped my life in uncountable ways.

Note on the Translation

Japanese names in this book appear in the traditional order, with the surname before the personal name.

The translations of all poems published before the 1990s are based on *Teihon Tada Chimako shishū* [*The Authoritative Edition of the Poetry of Tada Chimako*], 1994. The translations of more recent poems are based on the various book-length collections identified in the table of contents and the bibliography.

Introduction

Soon after Tada Chimako died in 2003, her friend the feminist poet Shiraishi Kazuko wrote an article for a Japanese newspaper in which she called Tada "a goddess of intellect and beauty."[1] Although grandiose, Shiraishi's description reflects the position that Tada came to occupy in the Japanese poetic world over the course of her long career. For nearly fifty years, Tada was, if not a goddess, a solitary visionary who lived in an almost constant state of communion with the spirits of nature and the imagination, drinking daily from the fount of aesthetics and the intellect.

Tada was born in 1930, and her childhood and early adolescence in Tokyo overlapped with the years when the army was busily expanding the Japanese empire. For Tada, the events on the Asian mainland were secondary to her first days in school and her early discovery of books. During her youth, she read incessantly, and she delved especially deeply into the Greek, Chinese, and Japanese classics. As a result, the worlds described in those centuries-old works seemed, ironically, closer to her life than the dramatic events that were taking place on the world stage. It was also about this time that she made her first attempts at writing, attempts that were deeply influenced by the classical stories and *nō* rhythms she absorbed from her readings.

In 1945, the last year of World War II, the Allied forces began bombing raids on Tokyo and other Japanese cities, forcing their inhabitants to flee to the countryside or risk their lives as the cities were reduced to rubble. Tada's mother evacuated her fifteen-year-old daughter to rural Shiga prefecture, where her own parents were. There, Tada spent half a year in a small, idyllic town on the banks of the Aichi River. When Tada later reflected on this strange sojourn, she noted that her experience was far different from that of the majority of the Japanese population. In that last momentous year of the war, as cities burned across Japan and countless people died, she experienced a strangely paradisiacal existence. The local school had been transformed into a factory for military goods, so there were no classes for which she was forced to study. She knew next to no one in the town, and since she was left without playmates or pastimes, she turned to her books for stimulation and comfort. Books ignited her imagination, and when she was not immersed in reading, she explored the fields and river near her home. Even though there were soldiers in the town recuperating from their injuries, she had only minimal contact with them, and so the war seemed very far away.[2] Tada likened her months there to the sojourn of the mythic Chinese fisherman in the "Peach Blossom Spring," a mysterious hidden paradise. (Tada wrote several poems about her memories of the "Peach Blossom Spring" and her failed attempt to return there later in life.)

This stay in paradise did not last. Tada returned to Tokyo and the ruins of the metropolis. Some poets born around the same time as Tada were so profoundly shaped by their experiences in the burned-out wastelands of the postwar cities that loss, trauma, and nihilism became the base for much of their subsequent writing. For instance, much of the work of Ayukawa Nobuo, a poet who was ten years Tada's senior and who shaped the destiny of postwar poetry with his magazine *Arechi* [*The Wasteland*], deals with these themes extensively. Tada, however, took an entirely different approach. In the years of poverty and national reconstruction that followed the war, she retreated once again into the world of books, choosing the world of the classics over the ruin that surrounded her. By this time, she was studying French, and so she read Paul Valéry and enjoyed the sounds of Stéphane Mallarmé, whose lyricism she heard in compositions by Claude Debussy. In 1948, she began attending Tokyo Woman's Christian University, where she studied French literature, thus deepening her knowledge of French writing and stylistics.

In 1956, Tada published her first collection of poetry, *Hanabi* [*Fireworks*]. She had graduated and since 1954 had been a member of the coterie magazine *Mitei* [*Undecided*], where she had the opportunity to interact with many avant-garde poets and writers. As one can see from the translations from *Fireworks* in this volume, these poems grew from the rich soil of Tada's imagination, fertilized by an interest in the classical world and watered by the lyricism of French poetry. "Kodai no koi" ["Ancient Love"], for instance, describes an image one might find in a mosaic left from the ancient Mediterranean, and "Epitaph" is told from the point of view of an ancient Greek imploring a fellow traveler to convey the news of the death of a beautiful young man to Sparta.

The same year that Tada published *Fireworks* she left Tokyo, the artistic epicenter of Japan. Since at least the nineteenth century, Tokyo had been the place where visual artists, writers, poets, and translators congregated to discuss new ideas and forge new artistic movements. Likewise, Tokyo was the epicenter of Japan's publishing industry, a place writers went to make the connections that would propel them to prominence. Just at the moment her career was starting, however, Tada left, and with her new husband, moved to Kobe, a port city located in the Kansai region of western Japan. Less than an hour from Kyoto and Osaka by train, Kobe is home to a distinct local culture—one that is relatively international and cosmopolitan thanks to its ports, international trading, and colorful Chinatown. In the years before World War II, several prominent avant-garde authors who had settled in Kobe and the neighboring city of Ashiya gave birth to the loose-knit movement sometimes known as "Kobe modernism," which celebrated the city's cosmopolitan culture and local flair. These included the novelist Tanizaki Jun'ichirō, the modernist innovator Inagaki Taruho, the experimental poet Takenaka Iku, and the haiku poet Saitō Sanki. In short, Kobe had a rich literary past, but by the time Tada settled there in the 1950s, most of these authors had left and the literary scene had grown quite sleepy.

In Kobe, Tada focused more on her personal life than on working to become part of what local literary scene there happened to be. She and her husband settled into a quiet home on the sharply sloping terrain where the city streets, unable to climb the sloping base of Mt. Rokkō any higher, begin to give way to forest. She lived on that same picturesque plot of land for more than four decades. With a view of the spectacular city harbor spread below and the forested mountain stretching overhead, Tada enjoyed an existence that was literally halfway between the human realm and the world of nature. Although in private conversations she sometimes expressed regret that she lived so far from Tokyo, the center of the Japanese poetic world, Tada cultivated her position at the edge of the poetic mainstream, where she could create at her own pace. From the study where she did much of her writing, she could listen to the quiet gurgling of the small river that flowed down the mountain directly behind her home, and snakes and wild boars from the nearby woods would wander into her garden as if to keep her company.

Given this existence, it is perhaps no wonder that the motifs of rivers, trees, and animals recur countless times in Tada's writing. Still, when she writes of these things, they are more than just simple natural phenomena; they resonate with mythological and archetypal significance. For instance, in "Hotaru" ["Firefly"] or "Kawa no hotori ni" ["Along the Riverbank"], rivers serve as Stygian barriers that separate the world of the living present from the ghostly realm of the unknown. Likewise, the image of the river as a barrier between the world of the living and the realm of the dead recurs in *Nagai kawa no aru kuni* [*The Land of the Long River*], an entire collection of poems inspired by Tada's journeys—both actual and imaginary—through Egypt. The use of this kind of archetypal imagery reflects Tada's lifelong passion for mythology and ancient thought, especially that of the ancient Mediterranean and Near East. Later in life, Tada traveled to places steeped in myth and history, such as Greece, Italy, Egypt, and Mexico. Not surprisingly, these journeys provided the inspiration for many new poems, some of which appear in this collection of translations.

Tada believed that for poets to be relevant to society and the world in general, they should be familiar with the archetypes, ideas, and currents that had shaped human thinking over the centuries. Indeed, this is one of the reasons that critics and admirers in the Japanese poetic world have often called her a "poet of the intellect." In her opinion, it was the duty of the modern poet to take a position vis-à-vis these ideas and to comment on them, thus adding his or her own voice to those of previous generations. Rather than trying to make a radical break from the past like many modern poets, Tada showed that the modern poet could use the past as a stepping stone—a bridge to the future—even while working out radically new ideas. In this regard, her thinking was in line with that of three of her close friends, the poets Takahashi Mutsuo, Washisu Shigeo, and Aizawa Keizō, all of whom had studied classical literature extensively. During the 1970s, all four became contributors to the coterie magazine *Kyōen* [*Symposium*]. The poems, articles, and essays that appeared in this literary journal, which took its name from the famous Platonic dialogue, often drew on classical motifs in discussing themes of contemporary interest, such as eroticism and existentialism.

Another factor that contributed to Tada's reputation as an intellectual poet is the particular form of logic that infuses many of her poems. She often took a relatively straightforward subject and analyzed it from various unusual angles. One early example is "Shokutaku" ["Breakfast Table"], a poem about slicing an orange beneath an open window. Tada imbues this relatively common domestic scene with a sense of horror; the orange, despite its perfect, round beauty, becomes a body that two hands, working only for their own sadistic pleasure, dissect with cold, surgical precision. A more dramatic example surfaces in "Kodomo no ryōbun" ["The Territory of Children"], in which Tada describes the games of children in a detached style full of pseudoscientific diction and pronouns (usually elided in more colloquial forms of Japanese) that make it sound almost like a translation of a philosophical or scientific text from some Western language. What makes this work so interesting, however, is not only Tada's choice of language, but the fact that she reads each of the children's innocent diversions in a profoundly adult way: the sandbox gives children a space to become gods where they can create and destroy with guiltless pleasure; the jungle gym forms a geometric world of inescapable hierarchy; and so on.

Often, the narrative voice in Tada's poetry switches perspectives in midstanza, looking at a single subject first from one angle and then another, producing an effect somewhat like a cubist painting. Works that use this technique, such as the often anthologized poems "Bara uchū" ["Universe of the Rose"] and "Soramame" ["Fava Beans"], are richly multi-layered and switch rapidly between mythological or archetypal images, objective description, and subjective commentary. In Tada's poetry, a subject often serves as a magnet for ideas that flock around it, engulf it, and in the process, show how little we actually know about something that seemed relatively banal.

Because Tada wrote so often about mythology and faraway, even imaginary places, many readers have tended to think of her work as less geographically and temporally bound to her particular moment in history than the work of her contemporaries who used poetry to document experiences close to home. Indeed, as mentioned above, Tada's approach is certainly different than that of some of her contemporaries for whom the experience of war and destitution served as the formative pivot around which their art revolved. It is true that Tada did not use modern poetry to make direct, incisive comments about her immediate surroundings, the demands of her own family, political changes, or the evolving values of postwar Japan. This does not mean, however, that she was completely disengaged from the world. It simply means that she found ways to couch her criticism of society in the less direct but perhaps more universal language of mythology and surrealism. A close reading of her work shows that even though she often wrote about faraway and imagined places, she could be considered a feminist writer, given her dedication to exploring one of the major issues of her time, namely the ways that gender and the expectations associated with it shape the experiences of women in the postwar era.

Indeed, some of the most poignant explorations of what it means to be a woman appear in her more surreal work. For instance, the prose poem "Tōi kuni no onna kara" ["From a Woman of a Distant Land"] describes a woman living in a Calvinoesque city that operates by strange rules yet disturbingly familiar logic. The narrator describes scenes from her daily life—a life surrounded by the corpses of family tradition, a life hidden behind a smiling façade, a life excluded from the commercial transactions that motivate the city. In the final stanza, we see the narrator gazing over a harbor and dreaming of boarding a ship to escape to some faraway place. This small, quiet act of resistance to the oppressive order of the ordinary is, needless to say, an important technique used by women throughout history to escape unsatisfactory lives in which they are caught, aliens within their own immediate surroundings. (Not coincidentally, the sight of the harbor described in the poem recalls the view of Kobe visible from Tada's own neighborhood.)

A number of Tada's poems deal with the experience of being a wife and mother. In the fourth section of the surrealist series of poems "Kagami no machi arui wa me no mori" ["The Town of Mirrors, or Forest of Eyes"], Tada describes a common domestic scene in which a woman prepares a meal of eggs while turning her eyelids inside out as if to pop out her eyes and serve them to her husband. (In Japanese, eggs cooked sunny side up are called *medamayaki,* literally "fried eyes.") Meanwhile, the husband waits, silently expecting this gift of vision from the woman he has confined to the kitchen. The theme of the waiting wife recurs in "Odusseia arui wa fuzai ni tsuite" ["The Odyssey, or On Absence"], a poem that explores what the decades-long absence of Odysseus might have meant to his son and wife, who were waiting for him to return. The poem ends with a note of resistance as Penelope refuses to wake from her long dream of solitude. In the story-like prose poem "Dōkyonin" ["The Housemate"], a young mother begins an uneasy relationship with an old woman she discovers living in her house. Although their relationship is never defined, the sometimes maternal, sometimes vaguely threatening woman seems to embody the woman the mother will one day become. Able to deal with this only through pleasantries that smack of denial, the young mother continues to live with this ghostly portent of her own future. Although Tada does not use the poem as a platform to rebel against the system that limits the vitality of women by keeping them at home, her attention to this system might in itself be seen as an act of protest against the constraints of decorum. Through these poems, she reveals a dark psychological streak of contemporary Japanese femininity that typically lies hidden beneath social niceties, sunny dispositions, and convention.

Given Tada's interest in mythology, it is no surprise to find that many poems touch on the role of women in myth. In many cases, she draws a different image than the ones students of mythology and folklore might be accustomed to seeing. For instance, in "Niwa no onna" ["The Woman in the Garden"], inspired by a garden statue of the Virgin Mary, Tada reflects that when the virginal mother was elevated to her sacred status, she was also resigned to something like the constraints of the coffin. In "Genhin arui wa hitsuji no tani" ["The Mysterious Woman of the Shadows, or the Valley of Sheep"], she presents a radically new image of the mysterious "shadowy" female that appears in the Taoist classic the *Dao de jing* of Lao Zi, emphasizing the wrenching emotional and physical pain of the woman resigned to little more than the position of birth-giver.

Other poems do not disturb the mythological treatment of women as much as draw out the humanity of the women who have been described in myth and folklore. For instance, "Mei" ["Netherworld"] tells of the ancient Egyptian goddess Isis, who devotedly reassembled the corpse of her dismembered husband Osiris only to find to her dismay that he would never escape the realm of the dead. "Akebono" ["Dawn"] speaks of the Egyptian goddess Nut, who stretches herself over the firmament and gives birth to the sun each day in an unending cycle of labor. At other moments, such as in "Yamanba," in which Tada celebrates the earthy mountain witches who, according to Japanese folklore, chose to live on the edges of villages away from humanity, she attempts to rehabilitate figures folklore has decried as monstrous. Again, Tada uses the universal language of myth to uncover aspects of women's existence long relegated to the margins by concern for decency and decorum. One cannot help but see these poems as voicing a subtle protest against an oppressive system of gender roles that has far too often locked women in constraining categories, most often those of mother and caregiver or—if they refused to abide by convention—outcast.

So far, all the poems to which this introduction has alluded are in the genre of *shi*, a genre that developed in the late nineteenth century to distinguish longer forms of verse from traditional Japanese forms, such as the tanka and the haiku. (Before the nineteenth century, the word *shi* referred to classical Chinese verse, which had its own set of rules and conventions regarding meter, sound, and diction, but in the nineteenth century, Japanese poets borrowed this word to refer to a new genre of verse that emerged under the influence of Western verse. This word was apparently chosen partly because classical Chinese *shi* tended to be long like Western verse and partly because the term implied a contradistinction with indigenous Japanese genres of poetry.) Even today, poets are identified in Japan as either *shijin* (poets who work in *shi* or what some Western scholars have called "the international style"), *kajin* (poets of tanka), or *haijin* (poets of haiku). There exists no single word for a poet who works in all three genres. This helps contribute to the strong sense that *shi* and traditional Japanese verse represent profoundly different types of writing. Relatively few poets cross the boundaries of poetic genre, and when they do, they usually only dabble.

Tada, however, is one of the relatively rare modern Japanese poets who mastered not only free-form poetry but traditional verse as well. The haiku, a short form of metered verse typically written in the pattern of 5–7–5 morae, is probably the form of Japanese poetry most familiar to Western audiences. The haiku, however, is a relatively recent offshoot of the tanka (the modern name for what were called *waka* in older times), another, far older form of verse usually written in 31 morae arranged in the pattern 5–7–5–7–7. Because the tanka is longer, it gives poets an opportunity to present a more complex thought than the haiku, which is usually little more than a poetically suggestive fragment. Perhaps for this reason, the tanka remains the most popular form of traditional verse among Japanese poets even today.

The tanka collection *Suien* [*A Spray of Water*], published in 1975, was Tada's first collection of verse in a traditional style. Although she did not publish any more tanka during her life, she continued to write them. In fact, at many critical moments in her life, such as the death of her mother, the death of her lifelong friend Yagawa Sumiko, and her own diagnosis of uterine cancer, she turned to traditional verse to express her thoughts. On one hand, these poems show her skill at writing in the stylized language of classical Japanese poetry; on the other, they reveal a direct, powerful, and distinct voice that is clearly Tada's own. During her final months, Tada asked Takahashi Mutsuo to edit her haiku, many of which deal with her battle with cancer, and distribute them to friends at her funeral. The result was the collection *Kaze no katami* [*A Souvenir of Wind*], which was republished in 2004 as part of the collection *Fū o kiru to* [*Upon Breaking the Seal*]. The following year, Takahashi also arranged for posthumous publication of Tada's tanka in *Yūsei no hito* [*Person of the Playful Star*], parts of which appear in translation in this collection.

Interestingly, Tada's ear for the rhythms of classical verse sometimes informed her *shi*. For instance, the final paragraph of one of her most frequently anthologized poems, "Kagami" ["Mirrors"], is made up of what appear to be tanka verses spread across four lines. (In the following romanized excerpt, apostrophes show the break between morae within a word, and double apostrophes follow a sound that consists of two morae.)

Ko'no ka'ga'mi bi'shō" no ha'ka'ba ta'bi'bi'to yo	5-7-5
Ra'ke'da'i'mo'n ni yu'ki'te tsu'ta'e yo	7-7
Ke'shō" ko'ku shi'ro'ku' nu'ri'ta'ru ha'ka hi'to'tsu	5-7-5
Ka'ga'mi no na'ka o ka'ze' no'mi fu'ku to	7-7

Literal translation:

This mirror, graveyard of smiles, oh traveler
Go tell Lacedaemon
[That there is a] thickly made up, white-painted single grave
[Where] the wind alone blows

With rare exceptions, such as the three-line tanka of the poet Ishikawa Takuboku, tanka are written in a single line. For this reason, the final stanza of Tada's poem "Mirrors" resembles a *shi* more than two side-by-side tanka, but it is clear that her knowledge of classical Japanese poetics is subtly working in the background. One sees this not just in the meter, but also in the classical Japanese verb choices (*yuku* instead of *iku*) and endings (*-taru* rather than *-te iru*). Nonetheless, the reference to Lacedaemon, another name for the Greek city of Sparta, makes it clear that Tada is painting a portrait in which the classical world and Japanese poetic tradition form one organic whole.

Another genre in which Tada excelled was the prose poem (*sanbun-shi*). Prose poetry has a relatively shallow history in Japan, dating only to the early twentieth century, when avant-garde poets influenced by Western modernism began to experiment with the possibilities of unlineated, unmetered poetry, something that had no precedent in traditional Japanese poetics. Interestingly, many modernist authors of prose poetry, including Tada's Kobe predecessor Inagaki Taruho, wrote prose poetry in everyday, colloquial language. These pieces typically sounded more like short, narrative contes than abstract poems. Tada's early prose poems follow this pattern. Like her modernist predecessors, she tended to use everyday language to present short, dreamlike stories imbued with a poetically suggestive quality. Some of her prose poems, such as "Setsuna metsu no neko" ["The Cat of Momentary Extinction"] and "Michi no yukue" ["Destiny of Paths"] have a philosophical, reflective quality, almost as if she were writing a nonfictional essay. Not surprisingly, the personal essay was another form in which Tada excelled.[3]

Finally, Tada was also one of Japan's foremost translators of French literature. In fact, her translation of Marguerite Yourcenar's *Mémoires d'Hadrien* [*Memoirs of Hadrian*] so skillfully represented the voice of the ancient Roman leader that when the celebrated novelist Mishima Yukio read it, he commented to Takahashi Mutsuo that the woman's name Tada Chimako must be the pen name of a male translator. When Takahashi responded that Tada Chimako was indeed a woman, Mishima responded—perhaps in jest, perhaps out of chauvinism—that no, Tada Chimako *had* to be a man. (When Takahashi later relayed this story to Tada, she laughed and said that she was not especially girly; after all, she had been raised on Plutarch's biographies of the Greek heroes and the Chinese classic of politics and war *Sanguozhi* [*Romance of the Three Kingdoms*].)[4] Although her translations of Yourcenar were especially well received, Tada also translated the work of a wide variety of other important twentieth-century French writers, including Antonin Artaud, Saint-John Perse, Julien Greene, Marcel Schwob, Henri Bosco, Joseph Kessel, and Claude Lévi-Strauss.

Because she was active in so many genres and her erudition was so evident in her work, Tada is certainly worthy of being remembered as an intellectual poet. But as many critics have pointed out, the intellect represents only half of Tada's art; the other is sensuality and emotion. Soon after Tada's death in 2003, Takahashi Mutsuo wrote in one of Japan's largest newspapers, "There are people who point to her poetry, essays, and translations and say that she was the greatest female intellect in the country. If it were up to me, I would instead say that she was blessed with both intellect and feeling. She was one of the rare people who would deal with an emotional subject with intelligence and an intellectual subject with feeling."[5] As one delves into her poetry, one enters a world of gentle stimulation that appeals to the imagination as well as the intellect. It is the greatest hope of the translator that you, the reader, will find this tender, cerebral beauty in the book of translations you now hold in your hands.

NOTES

1. Shiraishi Kazuko, "Chō-josei shijin-tachi yuku," *Nihon keizai shinbun,* 2 March 2003: 40.
2. Tada Chimako, *Jū-go-sai no tōgenkyō* (Kyoto: Jinbun Shoin, 2000), 12–16.
3. Readers interested in a sample of her work in this area can turn to the translation of the title work of her final collection of essays, *Inu-kakushi no niwa* [*The Garden that Spirited My Dog Away*], published in *Japan: A Traveler's Literary Companion,* ed. Jeffrey Angles and J. Thomas Rimer (Berkeley: Whereabouts Press, 2006), 117–25.
4. Takahashi Mutsuo, "Ko Tada Chimako kokubetsushiki shidai," supplement to *Fū o kiru to* (Tokyo: Shoshi Yamada, 2004), 5.
5. Takahashi Mutsuo, "Chijō minagiru gendai shi: Tada Chimako-san o itamu," *Yomiuri shinbun,* 24 January 2003, evening edition: 13.

Forest of Eyes

from *Fireworks* (1956)

Dawn
For N

The palm trees circle round one another
Quietly retracing their own footsteps
Upon the seashore gradually growing clear
The isles circle round one another
Dragging hems of fine foam
Oh, magnanimous, oceanic dance of dawn!
A rose-colored sailboat disappears into the deep sea
Chasing a sunken constellation

Ancient Love

Was it a sheep
Or a dolphin he rode?
Astride its golden back
The youth played his oboe
Melos unrolled her flaxen curls
And melted her long gaze
Becoming a delicate ripple
Parting the loose folds
Argos slid in
And disappeared into
A love as ancient as twilight

This Island

This island is an island without wells
The inhabitants collect rainwater from roofs
Store it and use it little by little

There are mountains but no rivers
There are valleys but only lava has flowed there
In the sandy soil, the inhabitants
Raise maize and potatoes

All day, the surf roars
The wind of the seasons flushes mist
Into the splashing waves
And the dandelions in the coastal woods
Wither under salty spray

This island has but one volcano
With a rocky shore at its base
The inhabitants simmer small amounts of
Seafood, shellfish, and vegetables
In rainwater collected from roofs

Night Snow

If you curl up and close your eyes
Like a hibernating creature of the wild
The snow falls, settling over roofs, both large and small
The snow falls, settling over the covers upon you
The snow falls, settling over your eyelids

And night falls, settling over night

Wayfarer

The drifting sand on the desolate peak
Pregnant with stone finally ends
By now, the king's castle is far but
Few hours and kalpas have accumulated
The Buddhist priest has turned his head once again
And departed from beneath his twilight tree

Vestiges of Storm

The break of dawn
The sea quietly dozes
A wrecked ship lying face down on its breast
Like a half-read book of prayer

A Single Lens

Spinoza, each and every day for your daily bread
You polished your lens, even as disease grew in your chest
You spent your life polishing the single lens of the absolute
Your theoria for observing eternity

Epitaph

Oh light!
Oh loud laughter of the sea!
Young time has been slaughtered

    Oh travelers!
    Tell the people of
    The land of Lacedaemon!

A windy morning
On a white cliff

    A beautiful youth sleeps here
    Body dissected
    With wretched glee

The tribe of dolphins comes to an end
The sun is already
A purified ruin

Tower of Vega

Carved around the tower of Vega
Which soars high into the night
Are tens of thousands of stars, each a cuneiform letter
—*Who carved this and when, using a sapphire stylus how sharp?*
These letters bestow their meaning to the desert and sea
Which sleep with closed eyes
Their meaning is quietly snatched
Like ice stealing bodily warmth
From Man who lives with eyes half-open
Pythagoras probably read these inscriptions
Shepherds probably read them too
And well as slaves rowing their masters' galleys
But inside the shining spire
Humanity smiles happily
Letting its meaning slip away
—*Who built this and when, creating this purified void to the zenith of heaven?*
We grow suspicious of the hushed, sanguine warmth of the body
That has failed to melt away completely into the crystal currents of air

Myself

I am planted in the earth
Happily, like a cabbage
Carefully peel away the layers of language
That clothe me and soon
It will become clear I am nowhere to be found
And yet even so, my roots lie beneath . . .

Breakfast Table

The morning breeze stirs the curtain
Flowers and fruit sit upon the breakfast table
Bodies waiting for a scalpel upon a surgical bed
The sun smiles faintly
A sonatina spills through the window
A silver knife stabs an orange and
Chloroform wafts through the air
While a hand devotedly carves the form of transient joy

May Morning

A child's eye   A green sprout shining with dew
A May morning hearkening to ancient days
A procession of black ants calmly
Crosses the pure white flagstones

A radiant, rosy funeral procession
Wrapped in flannel
The children let out sneezes of happiness
For they have conceived a kernel of death

Breeze

Like a loquat seed rolling over the tongue
The month of June passes smoothly by
When the fragment of ice upon her palm
And the sadness grown stiff with morning
Melt into the warmth of her body
The woman will clothe herself in the pale sky of evening
And all alone for a few moments, she will vainly, gently
Try to console the breeze in her hair

Wind

In the midst of the crowd
The wind blows through me
I am a pipe
And soon will be a sound
I will slide from the horn
With its shut eyes and
Blow quietly through the city

Contraction

Rain washes away the remains of summer
Autumn, dripping wet, crouches in the garden

Like a clam, my tongue coldly
Imprisons tender words
In a shell accustomed to the salty tides

I place a wet stone that reflects my eyes
On my palm thinly spread

My long gaze eventually returns to itself
Forsaking those memories that tilt and sink
Like a shattered ship in the distance

Withered Field

The biting wind of winter writhes.
There is no such thing as a horizon
In a mind where no one lives.
It is simply inordinately wide.
There are feet in these shoes.
How distant those feet are!
Today, I push aside the sun which reels with hunger
And exposing my teeth to the wind
I cross the withered field once again.

Ice Age

Glaciers approach. The pain of their perpendicular lines!
We purify the constellations, and all through the nights, we kindle
    bleached bones and wait.

FROM *The Gladiator's Arena* (1960)

The Gladiator's Arena I

The melancholic press together
In the round arena
Pull out your toy swords
And fight, slaves of twilight!
With one eye glinting
Quietly kill one another
In this ring of closed time

The Gladiator's Arena II

The gladiator's arena slowly collapsed
The stair-stepped seats, which like legislators ordinarily
Preserve rigorous rank, shook around
The two combatants with crossed swords

Preserving the reciprocal silence of conspirators
The rocks came apart one by one
And the spectators, with eyes still open wide,
Stretched their legs to the sky as they plunged

—Having lost all shape, the ring rose
Dancing upon the wind

Quietly, a bald eagle came to peer inside
The shade of the blood-stained helmets
Of the gladiators who had fought to death
But neither had a face
No, they had no face

The Gladiator's Arena III

Where many hearts were once stabbed
Now there are only the corpses of cut stones in a ring
Like a system of concepts piled high

Open to the sky, this ring-shaped ruin
Where both life and death are absent . . .
(A small emerald bird frolics formlessly)

Today, once again, the golden light of the sun
Washes clean the inside of this abstract grave
That has taken the form of a farewell from itself

Sunday

It is Sunday, when the beheadings take place
The park is plastered with ads, the grass shorn short
The elementary school students toss the heads
With faces like chestnuts into the blue sky
The fountain sends up a bloody tide
A street corner curves its back
And people whistle to call their little dogs

Execution

Slowly, slowly the man inhales
His thick chest swells
His thick arms rise
The shining axe rises
Into the blue sky
The shining axe rises
Into the blue sky where the birds fly

Beneath the man's feet is a tiny head
A thin neck, a chest, two legs
The axe takes aim and holds
Holds in the blue sky where the birds fly
In that moment the whole world holds silent
And look! The thin white neck slides forward
Extending beneath the upheld axe
Fleeing from the bound body
The thin white neck slides forward into the distance of infinity

Fireworks in Morning

One rosy morning
Chewing stale chewing gum
I took a walk by the sea

On the sand, a crooked stone statue stood in my way
A young hermit crab in its borrowed shell
Scratched at the statue's cracked heel

From between my clenched fingers
The sand leaked its dreams of sand, losing itself
An urn for human ashes lay on its side, mouth open
Drinking incessantly of the too-dry wind

With no thought of one another
Islands dotted the deep sea
While now and again, in a moment of oblivion
Pure white fireworks rose into the air

Legend of the Snow

And then, the snow finally started to fall
After the wind and rain and sand

Stopping all the clocks in the town
The snow slowly accumulated
Upon the towers of ill will
Upon the ramparts of mistrust
Upon the ruts of wheels mired in black mud

Wrapped in a cocoon of snow
The town became legend
A grave of white pumice riddled with holes bored
By spirits the shape of glowworms . . .
(No matter how sick and worn
The old all become beautiful with death)

Where was reconciliation?
The town of mankind forgot its weight
And sent a precarious bloom
Atop a single trembling stalk
Where it continually unfolded, petal after white petal
(Like a deep and gentle wound
That becomes the stage for the divine)

Where was prayer?
After the wind and rain and sand
The snow finally began to fall
Blanketing white nights with white days
Without end

From a Woman of a Distant Land

1

In this country, we do not bury the dead. We enclose them like dolls in glass cases and decorate our houses with them.

People, especially the cultivated ones from old families, live surrounded by multitudes of dignified dead. Our living rooms and parlors, even our dining rooms and our bedrooms, are filled with our ancestors in glass cases. When the rooms become too full, we use the cases for furniture.

On top of where my twenty-five-year-old great-grandmother lies, beautiful and buried in flowers, we line up the evening soup bowls.

2

We do not sing in chorus. When four people gather, we weave together four different melodies. This is what we call a relationship. Such encounters are always a sort of entanglement. When these entanglements come loose, we scatter in four directions, sometimes with relief, sometimes at wit's end.

3

I wrote that we scatter in four directions, but I did not mean that we merely return home, scattering from one another like rays of light radiating from a single source.

When there is no more need to be together, we scatter in four different directions, but none of us ever breaks the horizon with our tread.

Because people are afraid at the thought of their feet leaving the earth, we turn around one step before reaching the horizon. After thirty years, those faces we wished to see never again enter our fields of vision.

4

In this country, everyone fears midday. In the daytime, the dead are too dead. Bathed in the sharp view of the sun, our skin crawls, and we shudder.

When the nights, vast and deaf, vast and blind, descend with size great enough to fill the distances between us, we remove our corsets and breathe with relief. When we lie down to sleep at the bottom of the darkness, we are nearly as content as the corpses around us.

5

The sight of fresh new leaves scares us. Who is to say that those small buds raising their faces upon the branches are not our own nipples? Who is to say that the soft, double blades of grass stretching from the wet earth are not the slightly parted lips of a boy?

6

In the springtime, when green begins to invade our world, there is no place for us to take refuge outside, and so we hide in the deepest, darkest recesses of our houses. Sometimes we crane our necks from where we hide between our dead brothers, and we gaze at the green hemisphere swelling before our eyes. We are troubled by many fevers; we live with thermometers tucked under our arms.

Do you know what it means to be a woman, especially to be a woman in this country, during the spring?

When I was fifteen, becoming a woman frightened me. When I was eighteen, being a woman struck me as loathsome. Now, how old am I? I have become too much of a woman. I can no longer return to being human; that age is gone forever. My head is small, my neck long, and my hair terribly heavy.

7

We can smile extremely well. So affable are our smiles that they are always mistaken for the real thing. Nonetheless, if by some chance our smiles should go awry, we fall into a terrible state. Our jaws slacken, and our faces disintegrate into so many parts.

When this happens, we cover our faces with our handkerchiefs and withdraw. Shutting ourselves alone in a room, we wait quietly until our natural grimace returns.

8

During our meals, sometimes a black, glistening insect will dart diagonally across the table. People know perfectly well where this giant insect comes from. When it dashes between the salad and the loaf of bread, people fall silent for a moment, then continue as if nothing had happened.

The insect has no name. That is because nobody has ever dared talk about it.

9

Three times each day, all of the big buildings sound sirens. The elementary schools, theaters, and even the police stations raise a long wail like that of a chained beast suffering from terrible tedium.

No matter where one is in this country, one cannot escape this sound—not even if one is making love, not even if one is peering into the depths of a telescope.

Yes, there are many telescopes in this country. There is always a splendid telescope at each major intersection in town. People here like to see things outside of their own country. Every day many people, while looking through the lens of one of these telescopes, are struck by stray cars and killed.

10

When the faint aroma of the tide wafts upon the wind into town, people remember that this country lies by the sea. This sea, however, is not there for us to navigate; it is there to shut us in. The waves are not there to carry us; they continue their eternal movement so we will give up all hope.

Like the waves that roll slowly from the shore, we sigh heavily. We throw our heads back, then hang them in resignation. We crumple to the ground, our skirts fanning over the dunes . . .

11

Ignorant of all this, trading ships, laden with unknown products, move into the harbor. People speak in unknown languages; unknown faces appear and disappear. Ah, how many times have I closed my eyes and covered my ears against the wail of the sirens while sending my heart from the harbor on board one of those ships?

FROM *Universe of the Rose* (1964)

Dead Sun

Spilling twinkling droplets of light
The child crawls upward
Into a world still free of furrows

He somersaults forward
The hourglass turns over
And a new era begins

He picks up stars to skip like stones
Ancient fish flap their fins and laugh
Splashing the feet of the gods

■

In due time the child grows tall
His memory grows heavy

The world becomes full of his footprints
And with a yawn
The child leaves for somewhere unknown
With the sun still stuck, dead, in his pocket

Darkness

In the pitch-black night sky
The roses grow full
Tens of thousands of them wriggle in the darkness
I know the heavy nighttime dew
Falling on the nape of my neck
Is the sweat of the roses as they crowd together

Universe of the Rose
Lysergic acid diethylamide

> Although completely invisible to the naked eye, each of these microscopic points and lines is a world complete in and of itself, and therefore, size and density exist there in precisely inverse proportion to one another.
>
> NICHOLAS OF CUSA

Prologue

A single rose—
Here one finds the full range of crimson hues
The petals of gradated color are chains of being
That connect earth to heaven, past to future
With a glissando, I descend the scale
And inside the folds of the unborn petals
I catch a glimpse of him, the great source of movement, hidden with his many eyes
An immortal spider who weaves his web toward infinity...

Universe of the Rose

A single rose—the universe revolving continuously around the pistil of a flower
Writhing free from dense crimson darkness
Sevenfold, eightfold petals, expanding endlessly toward heavenly delicacy
Then from the depths of the rose

Arises a sudden whirlwind
—Words that had wrapped the flower like a calyx
Cannot withstand the strain and suddenly burst
Throwing their heads back and weeping
(The bloodshot compound eyes of the petals!)

The innards of the rose are a coiled snake
The scales of the flower sparkle as it blooms
And release the smoldering scent of pollen
(Multiplying spots upon the sun)

The millions of corpses interred in the center of the flower
Are spread in orderly overlapping piles like the slats of a folding fan
Gradually, they regain their color and stand up, one by one

Then, all at once, a swarm of coral insects emerges
From folds hidden in the shifting waves
And climbs on the flesh-colored reef!
In the midst of the ever-expanding universe of the rose
What entity can find balance and equilibrium?
(Hold up a polished bronze mirror
Before the pollen-smeared soul)

This flower, born of me and continually giving birth to me—
When I tread its colored notes and follow its spiral staircase
A swarm of countless butterflies rises from the grassy thicket of my hair
And my eyes are dazzled by the aroma
Meanwhile, the spider
That giant arachnid with radiating legs, hangs over my head

Oh, whirlwind! A funnel that capsizes
All ships and sucks them into the purple abyss
As the water slowly revolves
A net suddenly spreads to capture
A school of fish suspended in the air!

Then in complete darkness
The rose which has shed the withered words of language
Stands upon the scales of Libra which tilt decidedly toward dawn
And shakes its petals, letting forth a ferocious roar

Epilogue

The universe is the work of an instant
The divine dream is short
Just like all dreams
In this instant, infinity lurks like nectar in the rose

Even within the reconstruction of the everyday
All fragments are imbued with vast arrays of hues
Dreams survive the ruptures that come again and again
And the roses will embellish my bones

FROM *The Town of Mirrors, or Forest of Eyes*
(1968)

The Town of Sleep

First Manifestation

Inside the circular city walls is a town covered in water
After the departure of all gods resembling desire
Sleep dripped over it like a water clock, one drop at a time
Forming a lake in the ruins over the long years

Like long ago, when all the stones were warm
The stone columns measure the sun's steps from their watery depths
While the birds, like the gods, rise from the capitals
Inscribed with vertical dreams, never to return

The current inhabitants do not know the town
Like fish, they sink into sleep with eyes still open wide
Only passersby peer into the water's depths
And see the ancient gravestones inscribed with their own names

Wind blows through the water, reaching for stars easily extinguished
Streets traveled only by the wind twist like the strains of half-forgotten
    tunes—
Forgotten queries, unfulfilled responses—
The wind strikes the gateless city walls and perishes

Second Manifestation

Like a large bronze chalice offered unto nothingness
The walls of the town brim with sleep
A chalice with a lip carved with watchtowers and dark crenellations

Messengers who come here must never drop their guard
For an entire clan lost in dreams of animus lies in wait
At the bottom of this chalice of clear and placid sleep

Third Manifestation

Today, once again, the archaeologists will come
To unearth ancient consciousness
By peeling the sleep from this town of mirrors
As if lifting away thin layers of mica

Someday, they will ask whether they gathered fruit
Of ancient plants from this colony of the burnt-out sun
Whether they found the musical scale
Running from the market to the temple

Fourth Manifestation

This town is made of fragile musical scales
That rise and fall in aqua blue processions
From faded century to century
People smile with hands over their mouths
Afraid their teeth will fall out if they laugh

Though tall at first, the sun slopes like a leaning tower
In the emaciated wind, and women are treated
Gently like fragile white vessels

One day, an unexpected tremolo spreads over the surface of the lake
And the women, in extremes of kindness, crack at last

Fifth Manifestation

These stalwart city walls
Will not collapse under external attack
But when the sleep brimming inside roars like the sea
And swells upward as if in violent protest
They will give way, like an exhausted embankment

Now, however, the king is in charge
A king able to change dream into stone
So the inhabitants' sleeping faces stay gravely solemn
And the water level remains constant
Each stone trailed by royal shadows

    Envoi

Lightning
Reveals the silence of the long night
The small isle quietly capsizes
Somewhere the sounds of stones germinating
A frieze in bas-relief stretches across the eastern sky
And the lake becomes a receptacle of morning

Mirrors

The mirror is always slightly taller than I
It laughs a moment after I laugh
Turning red as a boiled crab
I cut myself from the mirror with shears

■

When my lips draw close, the mirror clouds over
And I vanish behind my own sighs
Like an aristocrat hiding behind his crest
Or a gangster behind his tattoos

■

Oh traveler, go to Lacedaemon and say that in the mirror,
Graveyard of smiles, there is a single gravestone
Painted white, thick with makeup
Where the wind blows alone

The Town of Mirrors, or Forest of Eyes

1

The town is nothing but mirrors
The mirrors are nothing but eyes
This town is a dense forest of eyes
In which leafy veins spread out wide

▪

The trees join arms and weave a code of laws
Shadows and trembling drops of naked water
Get caught in the net of branches that spread
Like the proud antlers of deer
Within the silent sprouts growing from the stumps
Are clusters of eyes already lined with glorious lashes

▪

Paths branch, mirrors crack
Feet run single-mindedly through
The town of wandering nerves
As far as Abashiri, as far as Habomai
Grit your teeth and run, but you are
Still caught in the palm of the hand
Still upon a narrow road to a far province,
Deep within a wrinkled palm

2

Numerous doors grow around me
Deformed children grow in greenhouses
Grandiose dreams wither within a single eve
Grass seeds sprout feathers and fly away on journeys
While in the factories of the town
Countless versions of me are manufactured, each in my likeness

This is my town, the town of my own eyes
The people planted alongside the walls
Grow tender tendrils of age beneath the ground

Then noon comes
The swollen husks of their eyelids burst and
Release beans overripe in their pods

This is my town, the town of my own eyes
Most likely, I grow from another tree

■

On the street corners of the town are inverted telescopes
That show the world in unthinkably close detail

In them, I discover a single angel like a blot on the lens
He has a musical score beneath his arm and passes by
Holding an umbrella with the same gentle swell as the northern hemisphere

There, I take a rose in my teeth,
Flare my nostrils and slowly breathe in its smoldering scent

3

In this small town, many murders happen each day
All the windows go deaf
Only killers walk the streets
All wanting to urinate

They form queues
And release their shining arcs all at once—
At least, that is what they desire—
Sometimes a police car passes
The sound of its elegant sirens trails behind
But in its wake is their boundless pleasure

Trembling with rapture
They wander the streets again today
Searching for a toilet to share

■

With each turn of the revolving door emerges
Another man, another petal
Torn from a white flower

Bodies twisted by the black wind, they scatter in the streets
In the shade of a thin electric pole
On the banks of a dried-up pond
Or under the eaves sloping over a holy woman
In other words, each time darkness falls
The police stroll by unaware, brandishing their nightsticks
While the bird of a thousand years sniffs out
A promising direction so it might do its pecking
The men of the petals—
They who are to be pecked—
Listen for the policeman's tread then
Gather to form a lily and
With stamens erect in the darkness
Scatter their pollen like light

4

Facing the mirror
The woman prepares the morning meal
She turns up her eyelids
As if turning up her skirt
She shakes out a flash of pepper
While the man waits, fork in hand
For the eyes sizzling in the pan

▪

Women who crawl out of the water
Are shoved back in
That is the clergy's duty
Purple arteries are grafted onto
The twilight family tree
And chains of white roses are woven
To connect killers
Those are the clergy's duties
With a patch over their eyes
They roll up their black sleeves
And shove back into the mirror
Any woman who crawls out

5

Long, long ago
A giant lived in the mirror
A giant with one hundred eyes who loved to gobble up faces
When he died
The eyes were sown like seed
And a forest grew from them
A forest that grew darker the longer one looked
Even now, sitting in the depths of night
One can hear his molars grind when the earth rumbles

FROM *A False Record of Ages* (1971)

The Odyssey, or On Absence

1

Oh Odysseus, you who trained the wooden horse of pleasure!
The scent of your impassioned breath made your wife swoon
And when the horse's belly broke each night
And shadowy warriors jumped down
Troy burned in Penelope's name

You who started home so long ago
Wearing the ornaments of gods burned to death
You are always a man between the waves
You are always a man shaded by the rocks
Did that seashell dissolve
In the clear, acidic sea?
How about the bittersweet pearl in the shell?

Is Ithaca trembling like a distant star
On your brow even now?
Is that small isle wrapped in foam
On your tongue even now—
On the broad, warm expanse of your tongue
Undissolving in your sour saliva?

2

His son grew up looking out to sea
Perched on the highest branch on the island
Every boat was the sacred barge carrying his absent father
That of the god who did not even need to exist to rule

One exceedingly angelic moment
Telemachus flew through the skies
And perched on the mast of a ship deep at sea
Oh, the waves raised their heads from the water
Showing faces like that of his thoughtful father
Suddenly the mast tilted
Like a scale that had lost its balance

When Odysseus finally returns one day
For the first time, his son will doubt his father's existence
He will plummet to earth like an insect with wings plucked off and used for bait
But that has yet to happen
Every boat is the sacred barge carrying his absent father
Carried to him by the tides bearing the seasons
Carried to him by the silver schools of fish living in the depths

3

Inside the lonely womb, inside the warm water clock
Your wife crushes the grapes, one by one
Dribbling the juice into nothingness
Thus growing gradually thinner
During the long months and years of your absence
All of the grapes will be crushed
And Penelope will no longer be a woman

Probably one day the thread will snap
In her hands, already thin from gestures of waiting
And the spinning spindle will stop
And you will step out from the shade of the rocks
The man who is husband and father and king
White hair dangling over your face like a breaking wave

The suitors will mumble and pull back like a retreating tide
In her wordlessness, white and wide as a sandy beach
She will stare with wonder at you who have returned
You in the sunbeams thick as a swarm of flies
At you Odysseus, no longer the protagonist of the tale

4

The carnage is over—now, for the music
All of the uninvited have been killed during the feast
By another man, also uninvited

Stepping over the speared bodies
You call the musicians—now, for the music
(Meanwhile Penelope sleeps)

The feast must continue
Tepid blood is poured into the jars of wine
Purify those filthy memories with water and sponge
Before Penelope wakes from her slumber
And now for the music
Now for the flutes that will comb her hair
Now for the harps that will relax her cheeks

But Penelope closes her eyes to all this
And continues to sleep
Reluctant to wake from her dream of twenty years

Grave of Hyacinth

The divine ice has been smashed
On the narrow shrine path
We tilt the hot-water bottles at our chests
To pour our rusty water onto the grave of Hyacinth

Underneath the stone a young boy
Melancholically awakens his leafy buds
We place our hands into the soft soil of the grave
And celebrate the revival of the earth, scented like hair

Long, long ago, this boy walked with Apollo
Pleasing as candy, caressed by the western wind
The going was fine, the return was terrifying

The wind unexpectedly changed direction
And a discus fell onto his youthful brow

Break them or cook them
And yet the eggs will still return
Colored eggs of revival
Eggs scattered over the ground
Oh young boy who returns to earth
This spring simply to die!
Come this way, come this way
This is the narrow path to somewhere
We kneel upon the earth
Cover our faces with ash
And pluck off the dark purple regret
Blooming from the bulb

Calendar in Verse

I who wait for myself
I who do not appear
Today, I turn another page of the sea
And toss away a clam that died with mouth closed

      A morning that does not break   A white shore
      A womb that does not bear   A broken oar

I who wait for myself
I who do not appear
Today, I turn another page of the horizon
And toss away a snakeskin that is far too light

      A morning that does not break   A useless parasol
      A suspicious chuckle   A cold piece of fried food

I who wait for myself
I who do not appear
Today, I turn another page of sky
And toss away the sooty stardust that I have swept up

A morning that does not break   A patch of teary grass
I turn them   And turn them
But still I do not appear
I who wait for myself
A world of imaginary numbers   A love without arms

Tulips

Stretching their necks high
The tulips stand here
On the black earth of the execution ground in spring

Guilty of breaking the bulb's slumber
Guilty of fluttering in the wind
And playing with butterflies
But most of all
Guilty of bringing pleasure to human hearts

For these grave crimes
All the flowers will be sentenced
Sentenced to shrivel like convicts
Sentenced to stand and wither
While still chained together

Yet the ones standing here
Are the worst offenders—
The flowers among flowers
Tulips who gracefully accept defeat
And stretch their necks up high
For the axe in the execution ground

Putting on My Face

Facing the mirror, I put on my face
Apply a thin layer of makeup
But not like usual this time, not like each night
Tonight, I become an adolescent boy!

A fifteen-year-old boy's shirt and blazer
A fifteen-year-old boy's slacks
Strangely enough, they fit me well
I become a boy just before his beard comes in

This bet I wager takes hardly any cash
Not even as dangerous as a bet I suppose
Secretly switch jack for queen
And all is well, no one will know
(Repaint a rusty boat and at the right time
The launching ceremony will commence
All eyes on deck focused on the bow)

No longer will I envy any man or woman
I do not need perfume or pistols
Just think and I can be
Concrete woman
Or abstract man

The night grows long
Preparations done, I am ready to go
Among people who are
Neither husband nor lover
Farewell, unfamiliar adolescent in the mirror
Until that boyish dawn one step this side of man

The Well

The old poet spoke of life
As he sucked the lemon from his tea
The life force is unfathomably ancient and long
But your life is short from the start
Simply because you were born
You are not a well but a bucket
The water makes a dry sound
As the seeds of the chaff-flower fall
Outside the window of life
Men pass through women and
Peek out from buckets
On the sidewalk
An autumnal maiden stands backward
Feigning ignorance—
This is you soon before your death
You'll be thrown away like rinse water from an old rag
(The poet throws away his lemon)
That is the only thing that is true
When the contract expires
The bucket falls to the bottom of the well
And the world quickly grows miserly
(Meanwhile, an autumn honeybee hums
Within the hexagonal hole of
The old poet's ear)

Shade

A dark elephant from a dark forest
Came to drink from a pond
As the Buddha watched
    (A dark elephant from a dark forest
    Has come to the pond
    And swallowed the trembling vision of the moon)

A dark deer from a dark forest
Came to drink from the pond
    (The deer has also swallowed the vision of the moon)
The Buddha leaned over
And scooped up the moon in his palm
    (Drink this
    If it will illuminate the heart just a little)

∎

More than two millennia after the Buddha's death
His remains have been divided endlessly
Only imaginary numbers can count
The tiles atop the reliquary pagodas
That stretch into the sky, three, five, seven stories . . .

As a bright person from a bright town
At which pond will you scoop up water
Since night has been taken away?
What vision of the moon
Will you find in your palm?
    (Drink this
    If it will shade the heart just a little)

The Territory of Children

Slide

Start sliding, and you will not stop. That is the essential point.

Not falling nor gliding, but sliding downward—that is what it is all about. The pleasure mixed with fear that one feels grows rapidly as one slides downward. When a child becomes an adult and puts on skis for the first time, he will likely once again taste the shock of sliding without being able to stop.

Start sliding, and you will not stop—but in reality, the slide lasts only a short two or three seconds. The earth is waiting there to catch anyone who might slide down. Stable boundaries. When the child reaches the lower boundary, he immediately goes round to the ladder at the back of the slide once again. He clambers up so that he might slide down again. Instead of the tragic ending, there is a da capo.

Ultimately, the slide is a solitary game. For the child who enjoys sliding down, other children are not playmates as much as interlopers who get in the way.

A contrary child uses the slide to do what is, quite literally, contrary. On his hands and knees, he crawls up the inclined surface, which other children slide down. For this boy, the slide exists so that he might invert the natural act of sliding by using force to crawl his way to the top.

Sometimes he collides halfway into children who are obeying nature and sliding down from the top, but usually they manage to slip by one another skillfully. As he crawls up, he spreads his legs wide and lets the children obeying the dictates of nature pass right through.

Despite those defiant few who force their way to the top, most small pairs of pants and small skirts faithfully follow the law of gravity and slide down the narrow incline one after another. And then, when they have finally all gone home, it is dusk's turn to slide slowly down its surface with eyes downcast.

Sandbox

Here, the child is God. He builds mountains, digs out rivers, and hollows out lakes. In his hands, he forms sweet balls of rice or fragile stars of earth.

By absorbing a little liquid, the rustling, semi-fluid sand becomes increasingly plastic, resembling clay in the hands of Jehovah.

The little *Homo fabers* fill their rectangular cosmos with their own creations. And then comes the moment when they resemble God most strongly—the moment when without a trace of regret they destroy the forms they have labored to create.

Swings

Ontogeny mimics phylogeny. Children hanging on the swings reproduce for us our hairy ancestors just as they were, swinging on vines.

For the child who cannot steer the swing even though he awkwardly sticks out his derrière, bends his knees, and jerks his arms back and forth, this toy, made of board and chain, represents the world that will not do as he says. When the swing finally begins to move as the child wishes, however, his face shines with all the pride and joy of a conqueror.

The true wish of the swings is not just to move through a fan-shaped trajectory, but to form a complete circle. Even as that humble platform soiled by shoes dreams of tracing a complete circle in the emptiness, it swings back and forth between its fan-shaped boundaries.

There is one more secret desire that the swing cannot justify but that remains constant: to fly off along a tangent into the depths of the blue vault of heaven, following the lead of centrifugal force.

Still thirsting for flight, the feet push forward, extending farther and farther, but the hands tightly grip the thick chains that connect the periphery of the world to the center.

Jungle Gym

This is a world of angles—angles and nothing more—angles that trace the shapes of cubes in the air.

However, because the angles are made of steel bars with thickness and weight, the structures they form avoid becoming complete geometric abstractions.

Here one finds a proliferation of segments of a given length. They extend north, south, east, and west. They stretch up and down. As they maintain rigid right angles with one another, they proliferate and create this world.

According to other myths, the world grew from the swelling of a four-sided bubble, but nowhere in this world is there any sign of a bubble-thin wall.

One can traverse this world without stopping. It is not meant to pen people in like a cage but to allow them to pass through.

The inhabitants of the jungle gym move between the branches, arranged at equidistant intervals, without letting their feet touch the ground. If they believe in anything, it is that they can place their trust in the frame, but here and there, the steel bars are purposefully absent, so even the nimblest monkey is prone to misstep.

Look at it straight on, and the jungle gym is a fragment of ordinary graph paper. Shift your perspective, and you see that hiding behind each line are several perfectly identical shapes—perfect shadow warriors that lie in ambush, ready to attack. The flat image is reassembled into three-dimensional space. Space appears, retreating into the distance.

There is no doubt that these cubes are equivalent to one another as forms; however, because of where they are placed, they sketch out a certain hierarchy—perhaps even a certain social structure. First, in the most literal sense, there are the upper strata standing over the lower strata. Also, there are the inner strata excluding the outer strata.

There are cubes that belong to the lowest stratum and that have the ground as one of their six sides. Meanwhile, there are other cubes that belong to the highest stratum and that long to extend into the heavens, but whose dreams have been cut short. Filling the gap between these two extremes is a middle class. This undeniable hierarchy exists a priori.

The cubes in the center of the structure share four or perhaps even all six sides with their neighbors. These cubes are members of a perfect community. Others on the periphery have between one and five sides facing outward. These cubes expose their faces to the empty wind of the outer world. Depending on the number of exposed sides, they feel a lesser or greater degree of danger of being ostracized from the community, and so, corroded by solitude, they exist in their own tenuous solidarity.

This is a world of plurality. A wise grammarian once distinguished between quantitative plurality and numeric plurality. The former suggests the concept of mass, while the latter suggests division.

Doesn't the jungle gym satisfy both concepts of plurality—quantitative and numeric—perfectly?

It is, in other words, a massless mass that can be precisely subdivided into equivalent spaces.

The jungle gym is a tiny fragment of a countable set. Although it yearns to proliferate infinitely, extending toward the heavens, it must necessarily remain a fundamental set always bound by the limits of the human condition.

Similarly, what I have offered here are a few thoughts about the jungle gym. These thoughts could, in theory, proliferate infinitely, but they must necessarily remain bound by the limits of my humanity. What I have offered is a fundamental set of ideas—a humble bit of equipment offered for the amusement of those *Homo ludens* who have tired of walking with feet on the ground.

Yesterday's Snake

> The three realms are emptiness, the work of the heart.
> AVANTAMSAKA SUTRA

I saw a lovely snake in a dream yesterday.
No actually, it was not in a dream; surely it was in my garden I saw the snake. It was twilight and a gentle rain was falling when there it was, in the farthest reaches of the garden beneath a stone precipice, the only thing there that was still white.

But today the sky is clear, and so the wet twilight serpent will not put in another appearance. The enormous gray-and-white-striped snake, encased in perfect scales... It bore a look of cool indifference and endured my stare without budging an inch.

(Behind me, the brook gurgled through the ravine with the sound of the deep.)

Facing the ground, which was growing darker with twilight, I whistled. Suddenly, the snake stuck out its tongue—or rather, it stuck it out and pulled it in again so quickly the eye could scarcely discern what had happened.

A pointed, pale vermilion tremolo...

The instant the tongue disappeared, the snake started to move. It moved very slowly, yet with each passing second, the scales covering its body quivered dozens of times, smoothly shifting the creature forward...

From head to tail, there were three wave-like undulations in its body. Without modifying this pattern, the back part of the snake would seem to disappear as it pushed its head further and further in front.

(Is this swift generation and disappearance what one calls progress?)

The snake slid into a thick clump of grass at the base of a pine tree, leaving me behind, standing in the rain with my umbrella—standing like a tall mushroom, leaning to one side.

Yes, it must have been a dream—a long, thin, undulating dream generating and disappearing.

(The splendid display of vibrato of the white and gray scales covering its body!)

This garden is not the garden of yesterday. It is dry and without shade, and the babbling of the brook in the ravine has grown quiet.

Still, there is no doubt I did stand there in the dark, illusory rain with eyes wide open.

No doubt too, at that moment, I was no more than another mushroom growing in the corner of the garden.

from *The Four-Faced Path* (1975)

Dreams of Wearing Collars

1

I watch myself out of the corner of my eye as I get into bed and fall asleep.

After checking carefully to make sure I am fast asleep, I remove the collar from my neck and quietly fasten it around the neck of the sleeping woman who is me with the face of another. Then, gripping the chain tightly, I fall fast asleep.

2

As I bite into the apple, I experience a strange sensation—the texture is not right. I have bitten into the head of a child. It is still smiling, even though I have bitten off its cheek.

I take the dog out for a walk. It pulls me in the direction it wants to go. Droves of children follow me. (I can no longer tell which child's cheek I bit off.) The dog pulls me into a clump of grass, and my whole body gets covered with burrs. As the dog urinates, I wait at its side, and if it defecates, I bend to take care of it. The children look at me in astonishment. What they are looking at is not my stately bulldog but me, collared, walking behind the dog that pulls me along for our walk.

3

The first thing I know, I am floating in the air. I float there lightly, spreading out my arms on both sides like wings. When I lower my arms, I slowly descend to earth. I spread my arms and give the earth a strong kick, sending myself lightly floating back into the air. This brings me rapturous joy, but then I find that I am only able to float about thirty feet above ground, as if I am tethered by an invisible chain that keeps me in this uncertain position. No matter how much I beat my arms up and down, I cannot fly like a bird swiftly through the highest reaches of the sky.

I gradually grow embarrassed at my halfway state. I lower my arms and descend to earth. As I stand there on terra firma, I stop thinking about ever trying to float again. Then, as if nothing has happened, I resume life like before, standing on earth and interacting with people whose feet are tethered to the ground.

The Housemate

There used to be three of us in the house—me, my husband, and our young child who was hardly more than an infant—but recently, someone else seems to have moved in unannounced. I first discovered our uninvited housemate about a month ago.

In the middle of the night, I fumbled my way to the bathroom, feeling my way through the darkness so I would not wake my husband. When I switched on the lights and opened the bathroom door, an old woman I had never seen before was squatting over the toilet. The small tiled room, which had no place to hide, overflowed with brilliant light, revealing her age and ugliness.

She lifted her drooping head, squinted her eyes against the light, and looked at me with a grimace.

■

The following morning, I found the old woman sitting in front of my mirror as if it was the most natural thing in the world. With painstaking care, she was plucking the gray hairs from her head and lining them up one by one on a sheet of black paper, even though most of her hair was gray.

"If you pull out so many, you won't have any hair left."

But the old woman was not listening. With eyes upturned, she kept gazing at her reflection and plucking at her gray hair with a big pair of tweezers she held over her head.

"I'm collecting them so I can weave a pair of gloves for the boy. Or maybe..." She looked at me out of the corner of her eye. "Maybe, I will weave a burial shroud for myself."

▪

I said to my husband, "That old woman gives me the creeps. Chase her out of here."

"You keeping saying she's here, but I've never seen her."

I did not know what to say.

▪

I called out to the old woman, "You don't seem to want to show yourself to my family. If you plan on staying, why don't you at least introduce yourself to my husband?"

"I wonder if I should..." The old woman looked at me. "But isn't the reason I keep my face hidden because of you?"

These words hinted at some sort of relationship between us, perhaps even some sort of complicity. I realized I had to keep my mouth shut, even though I still had no idea what we were complicit in.

▪

I do not mean to imply that the old woman was a complete nuisance. She fawned over my son and often watched over him for me. One afternoon, I heard her singing a lullaby. She was standing on the veranda, and she puckered her lips, which were as wrinkled as a pickled plum, her mouth moving slightly as if sucking on the plum's pit.

> *I'll tell you a tale sweet as an old pickled plum*
> *Sit in the sun, bask in its light*
> *And put out your hands, little child,*
> *Wide enough to hold dried dreams the color of amber*

Next, she sang this song:

> *Oh little boy, playing peek-a-boo, peek-a-boo*
> *But little boy, take a good look and see if*
> *The old granny playing peek-a-boo is really here or not!*

At this, my son would send up great peals of laughter from the arms of the old peek-a-boo granny who was not there.

▪

"Granny, you're really good at taking care of kids. You like them, don't you?"

"They're cute. Because the things that attract me most are the things I don't have." Saying this, she continued slowly as if singing or tasting something. "His cheeks are as round as steamed buns. His bottom is like a peach, and he's got such a sweet and sour scent I could gobble him right up!"

She was making me slightly uneasy. She anticipated what I was thinking and continued, "The wolf that ate up Little Red Riding Hood was really an old woman. Old women always become nasty old wolves at some point. No wonder the words '*wol*f' and 'old *wo*man' have the same letters in them!"

It took me a few seconds to realize that she was being funny. By the time I did, it was a little too late to laugh.

∎

While buttering his toast in the morning, my husband asked, "That old lady you were talking about, is she still hanging around the house?"

I tried answering with a little joke. "You know, she's the 'peek-a-boo granny' who isn't here." I had learned from the old lady that there is perhaps no way to deal with certain situations other than to substitute words for reality.

Fortunately, my husband just took my statement at face value. With a placid look on his face, he tightened his necktie like usual and left for the office.

Garden of Absence

A light is on in one corner of the nighttime garden. Illuminated at about five hundred candlepower, one grassy corner of lawn floats upward to the sloping base of the mountain.

Accosted by light, four chairs that had been sitting quietly in the darkness begin to flutter. The sunflowers, which quickly turned their faces away, do not budge an inch.

A cicada on the half-shadowed branch of the cherry tree begins to screech, then falls silent, as if overcome by a chill.

A small creature dashes over the grass. Something like a spider or centipede. It spreads its many long legs and cuts lightly across the grass, disappearing into the darkness just like a water skipper cutting across the surface of a pool of water. Who knows? Maybe it is a water bug, and I am standing in a lake... A lake of blue water on which the chairs rise like a mirage...

A black wind swoops down from the mountain top and blows across the uninhabited garden toward the sea.

Fireworks shoot into the air near the sea. A vermilion dragon rises perpendicularly into the sky. It then runs out of energy, hangs its head, and dies.

The explosion of the dragon's birth reaches me a moment after its demise.

The Cat of Momentary Extinction

A little while ago, a strange incident took place: a cat appeared out of nowhere and started running around my house as fast as a gale of wind.

All the windows were closed on the first floor, so it must have come in through a second-story window and rushed down the stairs, but by the time I noticed the whitish apparition, the animal had dashed madly through my living room and rammed its nose into the glass door that leads onto the terrace. The collision generated a dramatic crash. When I say that the cat "rammed" into the glass, I probably do not give a very accurate picture of how agile it really was. The moment of the collision, the cat immediately spun around and crashed into the door of the entryway. No sooner had I seen that than the cat rammed into the panel of glass installed next to the door to let in light. Once again, it turned around. In a blur so fast you could hardly see it, the cat dashed into the glass door separating my study from the garden. When it realized that there was no way out there either, it dashed into the living room again and made its way for the glass door. Its nose was already covered with blood, and bewildered by the illusory exits that presented themselves at every turn, its face was a fright. Every time the cat ran into a transparent wall, it turned around with all the chaotic energy of a billiard ball bouncing around the rectangular perimeter of my house—bouncing first off this glass door then that one. The sight of the cat dashing about madly as if caught in some dizzying labyrinth was so strange that it hardly looked like something from this world. Indeed, my house does have lots of big doors made of a single pane of glass. Cats seem to be able to see incredibly well in the dark, but perhaps their vision is much weaker in bright places, or perhaps this cat was simply so out of its mind that it could hardly see. In any case, it seemed unable to distinguish between the glass and open air. Unable to watch it any longer, I opened some windows, but it did not even notice them; it just continued to run around the house like a speeding ball of white as if its only purpose was to ram its nose into the glass. Finally, after more than ten failed attempts to escape, the cat leaped through one of the open windows. Afterward, I found that my floor was covered with specks of blood from its nose. This sanguine trail attested to the horrific intensity of the cat's desire to escape, despite the string of setbacks in its way.

In Buddhist philosophy, there is a riddle about a cat that is used to illustrate the concept of momentariness.

Let me explain . . . Suppose a cat comes into the room that I use for my writing. Let's say this was not the first time—the same cat came into my room yesterday and walked around my desk once before leaving. The main question is this: In the interim between the time the cat came in yesterday and the time the cat came in just now, was the cat the same entity? People assume the cat from yesterday and the cat from today are one and the same, but are they necessarily right?

This is an important question in the theory of perception, so important in fact that the Buddhist Sautrāntika sect split from the Sarvāsti-vādin sect over this issue. In any case, I think it extremely interesting that cats are used to illustrate the concept of the "denial of the continuity of existence" or, in other words, the notion that a given entity will pass momentarily into extinction, then, momentarily, another entity arises. Cats are common creatures, found just about anywhere people live. In the nimbleness of their actions, they display amazing agility, but this nimbleness is not just a matter of simple speed. Cats also give the impression they come into existence without your knowledge and then disappear into extinction, almost as if undergoing some sort of metamorphosis. Avert your eyes from a cat for a moment, and it will quickly vanish, then later, when you are not paying attention, it will reemerge out of thin air. Cats are the very embodiment of the idea of momentary extinction.

Come to think of it, a short time ago when that cat tore through my house as fast as a gale of wind, he did not stay put for a single second. He never adopted the mode of a stationary entity; he just kept moving about as quick as greased lightning, running from one glass door to another. After quickly zigzagging around the house like a billiard ball, he jumped through an open window. After that, he must have run across the grass in the yard and disappeared, but the way he vanished gave the impression that he had leapt into nothingness. I suspect that big white cat with the patches of gray was probably the same slightly dirty white stray who showed up every morning and turned over the plastic bucket full of garbage outside the kitchen door, but there is no way to be sure. Even if a white stray with a wound on its nose creeps up to the house tomorrow and flips over the plastic bucket again, who is to say it is the same cat I saw today?

Today's events transpired in only a minute. The noisy appearance and sudden extinction of the cat were certainly surprising, but after the cat vanished, I was left with the impression everything that had happened was all just a daydream. I did not feel as if the cat had simply departed after its noisy escapade; it was more like it had been extinguished from the face of the earth, leaving no trace behind. As time passed however, I was overcome by the thought that the cat had never existed at all, that it had been nothing but some kind of subjective illusion. Even the trail of blood that had dripped from the wounded animal did not necessarily disprove this hypothesis. If I felt like it, couldn't I come up with a hundred explanations for the blood on the floor?

A half hour later, my daughter came home from school. When I told her about the incident, she gave me a suspicious look and asked, "For real?" As proof, I showed her the drops of blood I had not yet wiped up. She let out a little sound of acknowledgment that seemed to indicate she was half persuaded, but to tell the truth, I had become even more suspicious about the incident than she.

Destiny of Paths

Branching and converging, our paths cover the earth. Paths we humans tread, paths infested with cars, paths for railways, paths of ships, paths of airplanes—like the web of arteries and veins that encircles a skull in its net, these paths surround our gigantic sphere, leaving not a single space free.

Perhaps the reason the earth is round is because it is surrounded by paths.

Start traveling in a straight line and go as far as you can, and you will return to the same spot. If you try to explain this odd fact rationally, you must, little by little, warp, then bend the flat land, much like you are bending the arms and legs of God. You must make the center of the pure blue sea swell upward ever so slightly, while lowering ever so slightly the edge of the world we call the horizon.

Once you have bent the land you inhabit and formed a nearly perfect sphere, you can mimic the words of Eratosthenes two thousand two hundred years ago—walk in a straight line and you will return to your point of origin, and the distance you have covered will be equal to the circumference of the earth itself.

∎

There was once a man who wept as he came to a fork in the road.

No sooner did I remember this simple account than I found it would not leave my thoughts.

I remembered this story as I approached a fork in a road in an unfamiliar land. I had no idea which way to go. A single tree grew in the fork between the diverging paths, and right at eye level, the tree itself forked in two...

To tell the truth, this land appeared to me in a dream, and it was in that same dream that I remembered the classical Chinese phrase, "Seeing the forked road, he wept." Even after I woke that morning, that phrase continued to weigh heavily on my mind. No question the story was from China, but where on earth had I read it? I guessed and flipped through two or three books, but still I couldn't find the source. I guessed it had come from the *Liezi* or thereabouts, but I couldn't imagine why just this single line from all of the stories collected in that book might have stuck in my head. If I had asked an appropriate authority I am sure I could have found the source, but perhaps it was better not to know.

Perhaps I did read this line somewhere, but maybe it was a false memory, and in my dream I had convinced myself so thoroughly of the line's existence that I continued to believe it even after waking...

In my memory, vast as the land of China itself, the image of the man weeping at the fork in the road formed a clear, solitary image and refused to disappear.

■

Yang Zhu's story about his neighbor who took his whole family and all his neighbors on a wild sheep chase just for a single sheep that ran away from home teaches us about the terror of forking roads. This story of the many forks and the lost sheep suggests that if you expend yourself in too many directions when learning, your effort will come to naught. This moral puts somewhat of a damper on one's high spirits. What is so powerful is the practical fact that when he came to a fork in the road, he took one path, but that led to another, and before long he had entirely lost track of the sheep.

One path is enough for one person. A forked path is probably enough for two, but if this path keeps forking over and over, producing an exponentially increasing number of paths, there is no way to gain control of the situation.

If all you are doing is chasing sheep, then you'd be better off giving up and coming home. But what if you are chasing something more important, something irreplaceable . . . ?

Moreover, is there anything more bewildering than forks in the road when one has go *somewhere*?

If you choose one path at a fork in the road, you must abandon the possibilities of the other path. This means that as people wander along their way and come to a second, then third fork in the road, each time they abandon an infinite number of possible roads.

People are always going *somewhere,* but what about when they don't know where that somewhere is? In fact, that is far more often the case than not. Perhaps they should first choose their directions—go right, then right again, left, then left again—then decide afterward that the new land before them is the somewhere they were headed for in the first place. Or if they choose one direction and stick with it every time they come to a fork in the road—turn right, then right again—then perhaps they will make a full circle and return to the point from which they started.

When one comes to a fork in the road and faces a decision about which path to take, one is completely free. And that freedom confuses and makes one freeze with terror.

Long ago, there was once a man who wept as he came to a fork in the road.

FROM *A Spray of Water:* Tanka (1975)

a single trembling
of black hair
spreading in water
hidden behind rocks
the roar of a waterfall emerges

岩蔭の水にひろがる黒髪のひとゆれ揺れて瀧鳴りいづる

dim evening light on
the base of my fingernails—
phases of moons
that will never wax
to half full

爪の根に夕あかりさし半月に至ることなき月のみちかけ

one narcissus
draws close to another
like the only
two adolescent boys
in the universe

水仙は水仙とよりそふて立つ天地(あめつち)にたつた二人の少年の如く

he who made his way
into the forest
at the time of felling
continually shaking
his hair of bronze

風と共に伐採期の森に分け入りぬ青銅の髪ゆすりつつ彼

the youth flashes the
white soles of his feet
and disappears
for the bottom
of the navy blue waves

少年は白き足裏(あなうら)きらめかせ消ゆ紺青の波の底へと

in the pale light of
string music
the river trembles
a fine filigreed ornament
then flows toward awakening

絃楽のうすらあかりに瓔珞の揺れてめざめへ流れゆく川

the darkness of the snake
coiling himself up
in the ancient
esoteric Buddhist temple
cloaked in deep green

密教のみどり色濃き古寺にとぐろをなせる蛇(くちなは)の闇

the round spoon
with the curvature
of a concave mirror
scoops out my eye
and swallows it

凹面鏡の曲率もてる円き匙にわが眼すくひてのみくだしたり

the harshness of the
sound of the knife hitting
the cutting board
as if to chop the fingers
into thin strips

千六本にゆび刻まむと庖丁のまないたを撃つ音のはげしさ

the hot water in
the abandoned kettle
slowly cools
still carrying the resentment
of colder water

すておかれゆわかしの湯は冷えてゆく水の怨みをこもらせしまま

somewhere
in this crystal
clouded with cataracts
lodges a pitch-black star
hidden from view

白内障病む水晶体のいづこにか暗黒星のひそみかくるる

putting on a pair
of round clear glasses
I see someone
wearing a pair of
round clear glasses

透きとほるまるきめがねをかけて見る透きとほるまるきめがねをかけたる人を

once again
I follow the dark corridor
seen in dreams
passing several
dimly lit doorways

夢に見し暗き廊下をまたも辿るほのじろきドアをいくつか過ぎて

a person with a face
like in a
Da Vinci painting
shows a wan smile
then shuts the door

ダ・ヴィンチの絵のおもざしに似たるひとうすらわらひてドアをとざせり

though I climb
and climb
the dim stairwell
I do not reach ground level
nor wake from the dream

うすぐらき階段を昇れども昇れども地上に至らずゆめさめずして

will I die each night
and wander
those catacombs?
the long twisting corridor
leads to daybreak

夜ごと死んで地下の墓室をさまよふか夜明けに至る長き回廊

last night I was
a monarch in an
underground palace
seated in a shadowy room
deep in a labyrinth

きぞの夜は地下宮殿の王なりき迷路の奥の玄室に座し

the slumbering
sky is purple
my grave will be dug
this night
covered in snow

昏々なる空はむらさき雪しきるこの夜わが墓あばかるるべし

there is a portent of
early death in those eyebrows
how I wish those eyes
were crystals
formed of joy

かの眉に夭折の兆あり歓びを析出すべき水晶もがも

the red of a
single autumn rose
asleep with the lids
of its many eyes
atop one another

おびただしきまぶたかさねて眠られぬ秋一輪の薔薇のくれなゐ

FROM *Lotophagi* (1980)

Lotophagi

Within your breasts sleeps milk of marble
Oh goddess!
I came to the legendary isle with weapon in hand
But I have already eaten the lotus seed
And forgotten all I should
When dawn, hour of parting, raised its rosy fingers
It was not you who rose from the foam upon the sea
But a melodious adolescent
Perhaps your son, perhaps your lover
Please ... give him to me
So he might throw me winged words
Oh goddess! Your nectar is eternal
But the spell of the intoxicating lotus does not last
Please ... give him to me
While I sleep and six dreams still form a circle
In the holes of my pistol's chamber

The Lost Kingdom
For the author of Book of Memories

According to one theory, the kingdom never existed
Only regal bloodlines remain
Like crumbled leaves, just veins left behind

Our memory is cut off
Severed from its roots
Must we descend into the Land of Roots?

■

As an experiment, close your eyes and become a citizen of darkness
Sleep will slide into the depths like sōmen, nothing to catch them
From the Cretaceous into the Jurassic
From the Devonian into the Cambrian
Will fall like Akasagarbha's white whiskers

(As I remember, it is in the deep subterranean flows
That the shadowy gods swarm)

■

At any given moment, time occupies limited space
Dotting this vast desert are countless kingdoms
But for this moment, I am king of a small country
Look! The lines of fate crossing the hollow
Of my moist palm serve as proof
There, one finds this limitless space

■

Wheels roll across the desert
Growing bigger as they turn
The brightness of the radiating spokes!
The roar of the wheel of the sun overhead!
Let me ask, who born into this world
Does not suffer the wheel's punishment?

(Imagine the shell of a giant tortoise turned over
The soft flesh and ovaries exposed to the sun
Imagine this is all a favor for the hyena)

■

Come evening, the water jar of heaven tilts gently
And the stars spill out
(Questions and answers circle through my cranium's celestial sphere
Two satellites destined never to meet)

Scrolls of esoteric writing spread
One after another across the dunes
Decode the lightning-shaped cuneiform
The purple cipher that smells of smoke

The spear I throw at the horizon
Will pierce me in the back without fail
And from my wound will crawl
A wriggling snake
Kings with beards of bronze curls
Will come riding sphinxes
Along the serpentine banks of the blood-red Euphrates

(Meanwhile, arabesques flourish
Single-mindedly over the great sandstone walls
A tangle of colorless, flat lines
Permitting not even a single amoeba to exist)

■

People who live precariously in their illusory towers
People who speak, eat, and sleep in their towers of illusion
Someday, they must fall from their castles in the air

But there, a young man bends gracefully
To tie his golden sandal
For him, life is still solid architecture
Death nothing more than legend

■

Let us turn dreams around
Reverse the tide and turn the desert into sea
All kingdoms sink into the land of roots
For that is the beginning of everything
The soul hangs suspended in midair
Looks down at history, drowned
And there I am, a small king of a small lost kingdom
Atop my head there is a hole
And with each passing kalpa
A single petal falls in

To a Retreating Figure
For a deceased classicist

Why is only your retreating figure visible
As if you were Orpheus forbidden to turn?

You walk quickly away
(No one follows behind)
A snake lifts his triangular head
From the thicket of saw-toothed acanthus to see you off
While rocking his forehead of jade

■

Your retreating figure grows distant
Moving along the rock-strewn path
Without a single misstep
(No one follows behind)

The path forks
A path sloping left, a path sloping right
A path sloping up, a path sloping down
(The genealogical tree forks many times
Yet has no roots anywhere)

You pause at the fork in the path
And your retreating figure slips to the side
Becoming multiple versions of you
Like a pack of stacked cards sliding apart
(At the same time, your shadow grows faint)
You scatter to all directions
(On the sloping paths)
I wait on the forking path
Hoping that someday you
(Like a god who reveals himself to travelers)
Will return to take simple nourishment
Among the living

(But in that dark place you have probably
Already placed pomegranate seeds in your mouth)

■

The sun has grown thin and small
Its light weak
Only half penetrating the empty space
Softly, lightly
Like the soul with nowhere to go . . .
(We watch
Upon the slopes
Chewing our mint leaves)

Boys of Summer

1

On earth where many bare feet have run
We boys stretch out
We exchange embraces with no one
But we are more complete than any future

2

We boys hang down
Upon swings at the height of day
Our slight yawns
Like a ripening akebia fruit

3

Long ago, we boys left a fountain
And now go in all directions through the square
The sun which has lost its eyelids watches
The same radiant dream over and over again

4

With the soles of our feet, we kick up waves
And we leave along the muddy shore
Our arms reach further and further ahead
Perhaps toward the deep blue of the ancient sea

5

Turning the earth with our father's bones, we spread young seeds
And cultivate summer upon cetacean memories
Each era gets its own forest
Each era gets its own graveyard

6

As if creating cairns, we stack
The corpses of cicadas caught during vacation
And with our butterfly nets over our shoulders
We depart for another, even taller summer

Grammar of Summer

A summer of assertions
Tilts its head   runs out of words
(Somewhere the sound of water
Memories revived by the bitterness of bellflowers!)
A snake returns to the thicket, the shape of a question mark

A halo of backlighting borne low upon his back
The boy's cut still spouting salt
Twilight descending   a great eye patch
(Softly you remove the plaster casts from the joints of dream)

Before long the stars will fall into rank
Until then, the reflections of light on water
The ripples of the eyes
The soul, only these will lead you astray

You, the youth with fragile lashes!
Spread your palms into emptiness
Catch the punctuation to end it all
(It will flash on and off like a firefly
And escape downstream into the distance . . .)

The Bodhisattva's Sea

Sea
Breaking waves
Unceasing
Bending the fingers of a thousand hands
The bodhisattva counts to infinity
"One hundred laksas form one koti . . . A koti of kotis forms one ayuta . . . An ayuta of ayutas forms one nayuta . . . A nayuta of nayutas forms one bimbara . . . An immeasurable number of immeasurable numbers forms an even greater immeasurable number . . . A greater immeasurable number of greater immeasurable numbers forms one inexplicable number . . . An inexplicable number of inexplicable numbers forms an even greater inexplicable number . . . "
Again and again, the wheel of samsara turns
Bending the fingers of a thousand hands
The bodhisattva recalls only the unknown
A dawn moon
Over the bodhisattva's sea of action
While at the bottom of the sea sleeps a cat
Its shut eyes the color of the sea

Waves
Undulation
And embraces
Silver dorsal and pectoral fins, whereabouts unknown
Shaded islands in the shining sea
Many-structured Buddhist temples send up their smoky spray
Over the endless, repeating waves
In the emptiness, the great wheel of dharma at dawn
Explicable and inexplicable by turns
The sea is in the cat's dream

Setting Sun

Across the edge of a vermilion-dyed field
The youthful Asura runs through
The final sunset before the end of life
(A single trail of smoke on the horizon
To burn the self in due time)

His swift, raised sword
Multiplies with mankind's numbers
There is only one Asura shadow passing through the emptiness
Making a slice through the purple wind that shines

Like a scroll from some esoteric sect
The earth has been unfurled
Upon it, our actions difficult to decipher
As we bloom with laughter once before death

Meanwhile, a stone stupa, sick with twilight
Crumbles with the coming of twilight
A gravestone of five stacked stones
Representing earth, water, fire, wind, and air

Dark Sea

This night, this night only
A single ship slips silently from the desolate shipyard
And glides onto the dark sea
To watch, I have left my mother's deathbed
And come to the shore after carefully preparing
The funerary incense by her pillow

The ship sparkles all along its hull
A terrifying birth
And an easy death
My mother's throat gurgled like the sea
(Once long ago, she swallowed the seed of a crimson fruit
And a sprout started to grow from her navel . . .)

What camouflaged god stands aboard the ship?
I watch lost in thought
By the ship's side is a giant fin
There is a trap set there, a bottomless hole
Whenever a starfish dies in its emptiness
The emptiness of the sky
It becomes a solitary star falling to shore of its own accord

Oh, no starfish—what cruelty!
(*I will pick the star up and preserve it in alcohol*
With the sprout from my mother's navel)
The gurgling of the sea suddenly stops
Right then, the deep sea's breath
Blows over me like a great strip of gauze covering my face . . .

Horrors of the Kitchen

No matter how tranquil the home, there is always one room of foul portents. There, in the midst of day, people brandish murderous weapons and slaughter unfortunate little creatures. Those who are already dead are flayed and chopped to bits atop the sacrificial altar known as the cutting board.

Blood purifies the cutting board. The reason that the board is washed with soap and water is merely to return the sacrificial altar to its abnormally pristine state so that it can wait, clean as white paper, for its next purification.

The chef is a priest who consecrates the corpse and transforms it into delicate flavor in the mouth. His pure white cassock signifies his priestly status.

Even the gentle knives used to carve fruit clearly reveal their murderous side when they stab the crimson cheeks of an apple, don't they?

In one corner of the kitchen is a white box that produces a manmade Arctic. They call it a refrigerator or a freezer. As a space, it has an entirely different character than the bright warm kitchen around it, and like the murderous thoughts lurking in the deepest recesses of a grinning man's mind, its fatal cold and darkness are carefully sealed inside, never to spill forth.

How the hand-plucked corpses of the birds and beasts stowed inside the white box look like frozen corpses lined up in a morgue!

The room is equipped with multiple gas burners where one can cook as one pleases. If one likes, one can also leave the valves open and the gas unlit. The kitchen will transform into a perfect gas chamber.

And when one places a round chicken or turkey on the broiling pan and closes the door of the heated oven, aren't one's thoughts drawn to the steel doors of the crematorium slamming shut to seal in a human corpse? Even the gentle gas stove in my home is enough to bake a baby right through.

One hardly needs to talk about the fury of the water placed upon the flames and forced to boil, but how could one possibly wash away the bitter grudge of the water inside the kettle left to slowly go cold?

Within the tranquil kitchen, the stack of snow-white eggs maintains its precarious balance, while a sharpened cleaver dangles like the sword of Damocles over the head of the chef working beneath.

FROM *Ceremonial Fire* (1986)

Peach Blossom Spring

Come out of the tunnel and
There are grave-like mountains at twilight
The peach trees are in bloom
Fathers and mothers warble
A child plays alone on an incline
Illuminated by the western sun
While an elderly grave-keeper dozes

Come visit this tranquil country village . . .
The bamboo shoots grow underfoot
While the new gravestones grow unnoticed
Just within the hesitant moment
It takes a peach to leave its thin branch
And dance its way to the grass beneath

Come out of the tunnel and
There is the world of the peach
The written word is entrusted to stone
And the water of the yellow spring murmurs
Reflecting the glittering laugh of the child
While the silver hair of the grave-keeper turns red
Dyed by the sunset of the distant past

Firefly

A firefly bobs up and down
In the darkness that has fallen around me
Who is this firefly, wet with light?
My own mother perhaps?

Fragments of music played on strings fall from above
Like dappled sunlight through the trees
Who is this? A bodhisattva perhaps?
Somewhere, I hear his jewelry tremble . . .

I have lived through many summers
I have crossed many rivers
(Miraculously, however,
The water was always clear)

But finally I come to this legendary river
Brimming with the waters of oblivion
A river of unknown width and depth

Who is this tiny firefly that has once again
Illuminated its tiny light? Me perhaps?
Silent as a punctuation mark
It illuminates my down-turned forehead

Yamanba

With flies that speak the language of men
She inhabits these mountains
Collecting innocent stones
And building aimless stupas
(*This is playing with karma in sand*)
Her eyes shine the color of amber

Each evening she plucks centipedes from the wall
And encloses them in bottles of oil
(*In ten years, they will melt away*

And leave perfectly clear oil
The same color as my eyes)

Sometimes she plucks a metaphor
An amaranth from the shade
And dresses its leaves for dinner
For fifty years she has lived here
Conversing with the flies
(*Shall I remove my cloak before long?*)

Butterflies the color of dead leaves
Return to soil the color of dead leaves
While the woman, the color of a corpse
Kneads earth, the color of a corpse
Into a doll of indeterminate sex

(*In one hundred years I will have crumbled away*
Becoming just clean, light sand
Both the doll and me as well)
Then someone will collect the sand once again
To construct another game of karma

One morning when heaven grows distant from the land
The cicada shell will shed itself and return to the wind
In any case, I present a flower as offering
The black lily blooms
Releasing its faint, foul aroma

The Woman of the Thread

By the small entrance of the labyrinth (or the world)
The woman lowers her eyes to her palm
Where branching paths trace their way to twilight . . .

As her eyes wander to the tips of her fingers
She makes an unexpected discovery—her fingerprints!
Perfectly they parallel the pathways of the labyrinth

Pulling a pin from pleats folded in shadow
She undoes her fingerprint starting from the very tip
And in the process, becomes a living spool of thread

—Oh you of the foreign land, take this thread
For it will serve you as a sure guide
As you escape from yourselves

Proceed along the curve of the bull's horn
Bend your proud gaze and move further and further inward
Stepping lightly as if at a masked ball

Such steps will follow the divine will
On the isle, the bull is color of the gods
And time bends in the direction of his thick horns

The blood-stained thread is completely unwound
And the woman without her fingerprints
Offers pure proof of her absence

The horizon peels upward and back
Wrapping itself into a spiral shell
Throwing up a spray and turning into darkness . . .

The roar of the spiral sea
Penetrates the pearly passages of the inner ear—
Yet another of the woman's labyrinths that grows transparent

In the inner sanctum of time where the shadow is deepest
The man finds the overturned boat that forms the ceremonial altar
(What was to be slaughtered before it was certainly not the minotaur)

—Do you remember this boat?
It is the boat that brought you to this island
The coffin that carried my soul

The pain stops, the bleeding stops
The woman looks, before the vast burning skies of dawn
The dance comes to an end and the world lifts its heavy mask

CEREMONIAL FIRE

The Woman in the Garden

That woman always sits in the garden
Next to the fertile spring
Surrounded by flowers and silent birds
That woman's backdrop is the afternoon sky, always splendid cerulean
A sky that grows deeper in the distance

That woman always lowers her eyes slightly
And the people gaze up at her
To see the children's small forms reflected in her eyes
Because they are reflected there, they are sacred
And because the children lodge there, she is sacred too

The stamens of the tempestuous swell of the
Lilies blooming beneath have been plucked
So their vermilion pollen
Will not pollute her virginal robes
Was this the idea of some artist or theologian perhaps?

In the spring beside her, the elderly and half blind
Come to bathe secretly during the night
So her amniotic fluid might rejuvenate them
And their eyes restored with sight once again
Might reflect the children who rise to the surface of her tears

She always sits in the sweetly scented park
Surrounded by flowers and respectful thoughts as if in her coffin
Behind her, a transparent crescent moon
A tall cypress that rises beyond this world
A dark tower of the soul

Moonstone Woman

The moonstone woman combs her hair
Blind even before birth
She lives only within her own light

There is the sound of an earthenware jar cracking
And water flows down a long staircase
Into the depths of a murky violet hole

When she lights a lamp in loneliness
She senses dogs crouching
At the four corners of the earth

The woman will someday go beyond the tower
Crossing corridors of gathering clouds
Led by fish with lidless eyes

But now, she holds sour fruit in her mouth
And combs the moonlight
Sitting swallowed in shadow

Ceremonial Fire

The world celebrates its beautiful weakness
Smoothing its hair which has gone slightly mad
Gazing at the melancholy of women, the melancholy of men reflected in
    the water
(How many relatives have been lost to its obscure depths?)

The grammar of pleasure already belongs to dead languages
Dumb cane, forget-me-nots (even the happy flowers of forgetting) all wilt
    so easily
The quick fluttering of lashes stirs the wind and ignites
A ceremonial fire, a purifying fire for all that proceeds to ruin

In the same spot where the emerald praying mantis
Once raised his emerald blade, an amber mantis
Has already lowered his amber axe
(Its sound reverberated round the world)

Mankind will probably enjoy turning to stone
Exposed to the sun and cooling in the light
(On the far shore, however, the breaking brainwaves
Will send up their glorious spray for time immemorial)

Fava Beans

I remember Pythagoras
As I shell the young fava beans
(*He was the one who said*
One should not eat fava beans)

Inside the thick hulls
Swathed in thick white cotton
They doze, green infants

Pulling each bean from its sleep
I cut out its closed black eyelid with my knife
(*Each bean is circumcised*
In order to be offered at the table)

The stalks of fava beans are hollow
And without branching nodes
They lead directly to the netherworld

The hulls are attached right to the stalks
Attached facing upward
(*He stated their hulls must not be picked*
For they point toward heaven)

Count the fava beans
Their number is the number of the dead
Their number is the number of living yet to be born

The pale fava beans with their swollen faces
Do look rather dejected
Boil these faces with salt
And put them in your mouth

The face of one who chews fava beans
Beneath the green shade of a tree
Takes on the tint of the spirits of the dead

Thief of Fire

Behind a stone farmhouse
Is a well with a heavy lid
Where flies flit about, buzzing while
Circling the scent of hidden water

In the kitchen hearth, a fire of white-haired charcoal
Dreams of glories and ruin as large as the world
While the old women watching the fire
Yawn and spin fragile threads

Having drunk his fill of honeyed wine
The god naps in the cool shade of the grapevines
The breeze pauses, wanting to lodge
In his long, unkempt whiskers

The dusty white road has continued
To twist and turn since the age of the gods
The droppings of dark mountain sheep
Dot it like some secret code

Ah! A man flees the scene concealing
The flame he has stolen on a fennel stalk
The celebrated thief runs toward the village of men
Where nothing, material or money, is to be found

Fragments from Genesis

I

Upon the white face of darkness
A stitched eye rips at the seams
And thus the universe begins

A cooled column of magma pierces heaven and earth
A lapping tide of eyes swells
Before the sun grows whiskers
Someone rows in from somewhere, straddling a green isle

2

On the earth, newly formed and still soft
A turtle drags its tail, marking future riverbeds

And in due time comes a master of geomancy
Who with his serpent-entwined cane marks
Where mankind should build his walled cities

It is not the master but the
Wind and water who teach the earth
So that the prosperous city of one hundred gates
Shall be entrusted unto fire one day

3

A raven's nest upon his head, a prophet steps forward
His eyes are tinted the color of flame
What follows are his words
Incomprehensible to all who hear

From what primordial ocean
Did that vermilion fish swim
Flapping its flaming fins?

It that licks up forests, beasts, barley fields, libraries, and theaters—
That greatest illusion which destroys all others—
The vermilion fish wriggles its way across history
Then disappears leaving purified ash behind
Every star and planet carries the memory of this
The world's greatest flame . . .

4

[*Missing*]

5

As far as the eye can see
Sand that preserves footprints
Sand that erases footprints

But the one who made the footprints has vanished
Caught up in the swirling sandstorm of an hourglass

    6

[*Missing*]

    7

[*Intermezzo*]

Wind is born between heaven and earth
Grass grows to sway
Hair grows to wave

Toward all that grows
The wind raises its wordless voice
The wind sets formless colors adrift

It passes between being and nothingness
It grazes all things and gleams

Oh mankind! Let the wind paint itself
Let the wind sing songs of itself
Wrap yourself in its meandering, singing, fluttering sash
Which unfurls without end

    8

The hills wear a necklace of pearls
Strewn of the white sheep dotting their bases

May this cornucopia overflow with milk
May it overflow with flowers, fruit, and grain for the gods
We turn to the heavens from here on earth
Where starving children die with stomachs swollen

    9

A rainbow stands tall
A rainbow stands tall, an octet echoing
Over the heads of those mortals born of earth below

Yet in this world
Are lands outside the colors of any musical scale

■

In this land where few plants bud
Yet where all rests under the watch of one gigantic eye
Two men walk together
One holds a thin bundle of barley
One carries a fattened sheep
The two brothers walk together
To the ends of the earth, strangers still

10

It is a tower without precedent
It is a structure without precedent
An unbroken horizontal procession of stones cut and carried
An unbroken vertical procession of stones stacked and scaled

The construction workers' coarse conversations
About the fine flavor of the goddess's flesh
About the soiled sheets she dries upon the mountain
About the difficult dialect in which the deity commands
Filter down through the clouds

Finally, they spit out the most blasphemous words of all
—*We are ants*
   This enormous tower we build
   Is no more than our anthill
Because man has shown such disrespect, heaven grows full of furor
Splits open and casts down thunder and flashing bolts of light

And even now
Millennia later, somewhere
The enormous anthill continues to crumble

11

[*Missing*]

12

[*Missing*]

13

[*Or Chapter 1*]

With each passing kalpa
Dawn breaks once again

Or (to put it another way that is perhaps the same)
For dawn to break
The wave of one kalpa must pass to wash away
The countless dynasties and civilizations which rise and fall in cycles

■

Preserving its crown of shimmering waves
The sea reflects the gods' most recent dreams
This morning, will the sea level rise unto its purple majesty?

The Town of Absence

There was a time when I kept guard over a town of absence. As there was no one in the town and nothing to do, the sole inhabitants, my dog Tarō and I, lived out our days strolling around the streets and napping.

The most elegant thing I did was bask on the grass under the sun, picking fleas off my dog.

Brushing Tarō's warm, tawny fur to the sides, I would grab the fleas as they raced across his white skin, rub them into a ball between my thumb and index finger, and then when they couldn't move any more, I would squash them between the thumbnails of my two hands. The hard yet springy, swollen, dark brown abdomens would burst, sending out a spray of blood that gave me a small sense of satisfaction. Sometimes, a white cluster of eggs would shoot out too.

I could guess where the majority of the fleas resided on his body from the amount of excrement they left behind. The base of his tail, which he could not bite, seemed to be a safety zone for these small creatures, and a large amount of waste, as dark and round as poppy seeds, would collect there.

Dogs' teeth are inferior weapons for trapping and slaughtering fleas, yet even so, they tended to find the grounds beyond the reach of his teeth the easiest territory to inhabit. However, after I turned this into my main hunting ground, the terrain at the base of Tarō's tail became far less secure for them.

I was living in the town of absence this way, growing ever closer to the sweet beastliness of my dog, when one day a small portent of change appeared.

Small, I say? Well, it was certainly small at first. A tick about the size of a small bean had fastened itself to the base of Tarō's neck, right beneath his chin. I tried to get it off right away, but the stubborn little vermin wouldn't let go, no matter how I tried to pry it off with my fingers. It was too much trouble to find a pair of tweezers so I let it slide, and the two of us—one dog, one human—fell asleep embracing one another on the lawn.

I slept for what must have been two or three hours. When I rose, the sun was setting over the mountains to the west, and the air had grown slightly cool.

I rose, sneezing, and found that Tarō was nowhere to be seen. Without him, I would be all alone in the town. I turned up the collar of my jacket and started to walk slowly, whistling to him to come back. Like a sad breath of wind, the sound of my whistling echoed through the alleys of the town of absence, then disappeared into the clumps of grass growing wild in the surrounding fields.

I wondered where I would sleep that night. All of the houses in the town were vacant, so I could sleep anywhere I wanted. Every day, as I strolled the streets, I would look at the houses, and if one took my fancy, I would simply go in to sleep. I was free to sleep wherever I wanted, but there was no house I could really call my own.

On the corner of one of the streets was an imposing stone wall surrounding a mansion. As I turned the corner, I found myself before a flower garden so beautiful my eyes widened in astonishment. The garden was surrounded by a low hedge. The house was just an old, small, wooden building, but the garden was like paradise, full of white, pink, and purple hyacinths that bloomed spectacularly and filled the entire flowerbed. The final rays of the setting sun, so slanted that they were almost parallel to the horizon, illuminated the garden as I stood there in awe. For a moment, the sun lingered on the flowers, then disappeared behind the mountains to the west. As twilight abruptly settled over the spring evening, the brilliant garden began to grow pale as if suddenly submerged in water.

As I passed through the wooden gate into the garden, I called Tarō's name once again and whistled. This time, my dog ran from behind the wooden house.

Like the old man of folklore who had a growth hanging from his chin, he had something hanging under his neck as large as a ping-pong ball. Upon closer inspection, it turned out to be the tick that had been the size of a small bean only a short time before. In the space of these few hours, it had sucked enough of Tarō's blood to grow to this size. Perhaps it was my imagination, but the dog seemed to be considerably less energetic because of this large parasite.

I'm not always the best at handling my duties, but I couldn't let this go on any longer. I went into the house, found some pliers, and tried to pull off the tick, but in addition to the parasite being so big, it was so smooth and elastic that the pliers proved entirely ineffective. Each time I tried to grip its body and pull, the pliers would simply slip right off. I could grab it with my fingers, but its huge head had bitten so deep into Tarō's skin that when I tried to pull it off, Tarō would let out a painful yelp. The tick simply wouldn't let go.

I settled on a backup plan: I would stab the vermin's swollen body with the sharp point of a knife. Convinced that this was a fine plan, I looked through the kitchen until I found a sashimi knife. With it, I tried to pierce the whitish sphere, which had by then grown an ominous shade of dark red, but the monstrous creature was surprisingly resilient. Protected by an elastic outer hull, not even the blade of my knife was able to pierce its body.

I tossed the sashimi knife into the hyacinths and let out a sigh of despair. I wanted to enlist the help of a veterinarian, but there was no one else living in the town of absence. Plus, the deep darkness of night had already settled over the town.

Tarō was looking at me with pleading eyes. I took him into the house and put him down on the prettiest cushion I could find, then together, we feasted on the ham and cheese I found in the refrigerator.

There was nothing I could do that evening. I hugged Tarō tight and fell asleep with him. His body felt haggard and somewhat shrunken.

When I woke the next morning, I found myself holding a tick the size of a soccer ball. The dog was nowhere to be seen. Somehow, I sensed that Tarō had not gone off and disappeared like after yesterday's nap. He had been sucked into the tick and vanished. The parasite that had lodged itself on the outside of my dog had, in the course of a single day and night, sucked the poor thing up completely—my entire dog was now inside it.

As I lay there still staring in amazement at the giant tick in my arms, I suddenly heard a confused murmur of voices at the entrance to the house. I had not heard the voice of another human for months, perhaps even years. I felt a nostalgic sense of longing, yet at the same time, I was assaulted with anxiety. Slowly, I got up.

A set of parents had entered the house with their children. Apparently, they were the original inhabitants of the house.

"So you're the one who was guarding the place while we were away? Thank you for everything. We're back now so it's alright for you to leave."

Alright or not, I had no choice but to go. I mumbled some words of farewell and was about to step out the front door when one of the children came running up to me with the tick in his arms.

"You forgot something." Then, with a mystified expression, he added, "What kind of ball is this?"

I gave a forced smile and offered it to him as a gift, but he shook his head with apparent uneasiness.

I took hold of the monster as nonchalantly as I could, and I set out. Once again, the morning sun was illuminating the hyacinths in the brilliantly colored garden. As I gazed at them, I began walking with no particular destination in mind. The town, which was ordinarily so silent, was now humming. I heard the sound of car horns in the distance, and a man, who looked like a salesman with briefcase in tow, turned the corner of an alley and walked into sight.

I thought to myself, *They're all back* . . . The town of absence had vanished. The place had become an ordinary, regular town just like everywhere else. Gone was the lonely paradise where I, the designated custodian, and my dog had slept, eaten, and wandered freely, going wherever our hearts would take us . . .

I walked past the inhabited houses that had suddenly started to reject me. As if carrying a ball to a soccer game—or perhaps as if to bury the corpse of a dead child—I walked slowly toward the outlying fields, still carrying in my arms the gigantic tick that had once been a gentle dog.

FROM *Along the Riverbank* (1998)

Labyrinth

I travel through city streets where right turns are prohibited
Turning endlessly to the left, heading toward the center of the labyrinth
Led by blinking stoplights, turning left and left again
(This is the direction of death)

Was I in a huge hospital?
As I dissociated the joints of language
I distorted meaning, left and left again
I clung to bandages unfurling through great white margins
Or to spools of string that someone had given me

Was I in a sacred sanctuary?
A single body reclined
In the middle of a roundabout misunderstanding
Upon a sterilized altar waiting for the scalpel
A whole body covered only by an eye patch

Kill or revive?
(Was that perhaps me?)
May those who have once grasped the knife
Return, turning back time so that
They may turn right then right again?

Round and round
(But it is too late for the world
The circulatory system is already riddled with disease)

Tending to Plants

As I thumb through the calendar
My father's funeral urn appears from the darkness
Its lid is raised slightly
And the ash-covered bulb inside
Has sprouted a fresh green shoot
—Just give it some light and water
  And it will be fine
Says my older sister
—It should produce a fine flower
  Near the anniversary of his death

Along the Riverbank

I stand someplace and watch
People without weight transported
From this bank to that
Only once are they carried across

The water is clear, finely textured yet viscous
The boatman's oar sends up no spray
Although the passengers are spirits perhaps
All spirit seems to have left them long ago

As if caught in a deep sleep
Their mouths hang slightly open
They need no water from the river of forgetfulness
Probably their memories are already long gone

The old women look like my mother
So I probably resemble them too
Standing with mouth slightly agape
A close resemblance like one dream to another

As I gaze on them, I begin to wonder
From which side of the river I watch ...
Meanwhile, a dragonfly perched on the helm measures
The weight of the vast afternoon on its thin wings

From Dragon Teeth Sown in the Earth

Like barley plants sending forth shoots
These men grow from dragon teeth sown in the earth
Outfitted in full battle dress
They compete as they rise
Little by little from the ground
The points of their spears glitter
In the shade of the stalks of green barley
And their ever watchful eyes shine beneath their helmets

A chest sheathed in armor appears
A thick shield appears

Enmity and fear forged of bronze
Also come to life with these men
Their legs sheathed completely with armor
Will soon break free of the soil
But in the end, will there ever be enough time
For these men to fight one other to the bitter end?

Above the heads of these men born from the earth
Heaven has finished sharpening its giant sickle
And is already brandishing the crescent moon

From the Windows of a Journey
In Mexico

The Snail

The observatory known as The Snail
Sticks its half-collapsed stone eye toward the heavens

Long ago the people who climbed this stately structure
To read the sacred writings of the stars
Were of wide flat foreheads
Broad thick noses and bronze skin

The Snail taught them
Time is a spiral

—Time is the dance of the whirling nebulae
A cyclone standing on the curled hair of the gods

Maize is strewn over the earth
Stars are strewn over the heavens
—We shall harvest when the time is right

And so they began to count
The twinkling stars which multiplied each time
They thought they had finished counting

But what they counted most carefully
Were the days that had passed since the beginning of the world

Although nearly infinite
Their task was to count time
Not in years or centuries but in days
(One mistake and the world would end
Along with the days piled precipitously high
In a spiral the shape of a snail shell)

Fervently they counted and prayed
And from depths of The Snail's bloodshot eye
They saw to the ends of the earth

With carrying straps across their wide foreheads
And bodies glistening with sweat
They carried the burden of time immemorial
And their bronze-skinned gods as they walked forward

Cigars

They roll up the wide, dried leaves
And pass them out to each member of the family
Men, women, children
Sit in a ring
Around the hearth
Squatting
Sticking out their haunches
Smoking their cigars
This enraptured family
Forgets about time

Until the perpendicular
Rays of the sun
Fall to the horizon
From the smoke-hole in the roof
The god "He of the Smoking Mirror" watches over them

Salt

A salt market is set up
In the shade under the spreading branches of the mango trees
As the broad-shouldered man grasps it, the salt squeaks in his hands

He uses a gourd to scoop up mounds
From hemp bags on the ground
He barters for an obsidian knife
(To cut the throat of the sacrifice)

He barters for a purple striped belt
(To tie tight around his wife's waist)
And he barters for thirteen lustrous cowry shells
(A lucky number, so that thirteen children will be born)

After the people have gone
He pulls a green mango from the tree
And bites into it with a sour grimace
Then
He pours his energy into grinding the gray crystals
That remain upon the floor of twilight

Alcohol

Showing his respect to a world of base twenty
He calls out the names of the gods of the twenty days
The day of earth, which is a crocodile
The day of wind, which is breath
The day of darkness, where evil spirits dwell
The day of maize
The days come sit in a ring

He offers a candle to each of the days
When he finishes lighting all twenty
He sits in the center

And drinks alcohol made of the century plant
The clear liquid penetrates his tongue
And slides to his throat like a water-snake
A god that warms the insides like a fire-dragon

It slides down and returns to his head
And his bronze face glows even redder
The twenty candles tremble
And all things begin to spin

The flames, the forest, the universe of the twenty days spin
With him as the axis
Until he collapses face down

How grandiose, the gods that make
The universe churn and collapse like this!
Praise them in the highest
A dragon's tongue in the alcohol

The Snake

From the wall of the sanctuary
A rattlesnake lifts its head
As it opens its mouth
A human face emerges from between the fangs

Did the snake swallow it? No
The people once buried in this land
Are now being born once again
From the throat of a poisonous snake

With the same faces as before
With the same fortune
With eyes of stone still closed
The base of the sun, made of burning memory

The Finger

*—When I sowed the corn
　I also planted one of my fingers*

The girl with the many colored strings woven in her hair
Secretly made this confession

—A baby will grow from it
  A human one or
  If all goes well, a jaguar child
  With eyes of jade
  When my belly swells three moons more
  Then collapses again

To harvest what is born of the soil
She diligently weaves her basket
With deft movements of the hand missing its little finger
Both day and night she sits and weaves
Upon her bed of soft palm fronds

The Couple

In the entrance of a house thatched with palm
Sit an old man and a child
Like two statues, large and small
Their broad foreheads, prominent, thick noses
Exactly alike, the faces of the same people

The child sixty years later
The old man sixty years earlier
Seated next to each other in the entrance
The couple looks long and hard

At the conquerors who come carrying guns and crucifixes
At the goddess of maize smashed by the hooves of horses
At the snakes that crawl from the smashed sanctuary
And now, at the buses that carry travelers with dollars and cameras
Through all of this, they look
At the Year of One Reed that recurs with such exactitude

■

In the village nearby
I saw the stones the size of mangoes
These two had carved and placed among the souvenirs
The god of Old Fire
The god of Young Rain
In order to withstand the desirous stares
Did they have no choice but to turn to stone?

The withdrawn old man and child sit sulkily by the shelves in the shop
And watch time as it flows by
Like dark water, like sand
And at times, like slippery blood

Revisiting the Peach Blossom Spring

As we travel back upstream through the valley
And pass through the dark cave
To revisit old memories
We find the land of the Peach Spring
Has become a field of graves
Where thin wild dogs wander
Villages of stone, forests of bone
Only one great peach tree still stands
Spreading its branches in the thin mist of oblivion

Shall we pass once again through the
Mouth of the cave into the waking world
Or
Shall we chase the giant peach
That falls into the river with its playful sound
And bobs toward the village of fairy tales?
Turn back and a rainbow stands on one foot
In the field of graves

Valley in Autumn

The snakes have all gone underground
In the ceremony of the mountains turning red all at once
The pale emperor of autumn reigns

We step from this bank to that
Traversing unsteady stepping stones
And coldly dampening our hearts

Is the scarlet that spreads behind us
The blaze of some furious funeral pyre?
Raise the rocks concealing living creatures
And there is memory, shining and slipping away

But we cannot remember to where we should return
So we sit alone in rocky shade, arms wrapped around thin knees
And inhale the aroma of former lives while
Simmering stew from the roots of old herbs

The Mysterious Woman of the Shadows, or The Valley of Sheep

This is the valley where sheep flow forth
Clouds flow forth, sheep flow forth
The valley a fissure covered in white cotton
That smells of amniotic fluid

> In a dream, Minister Li Gong walked atop a mountain
> And saw a wide valley completely filled with sheep
> The shepherd said to him, "Your Highness
> This is as many sheep as you will consume in your life"
>
> Some years later, Li Gong was demoted
> A monk read his fortune and said,
> "You will consume ten thousand sheep in your life
> And you have already consumed nine thousand five hundred
> Sir, you are safe, five hundred still remain"
>
> But then a gift of five hundred sheep arrived
> And the monk said with a sigh,
> "Here are your ten thousand, Sir
> I must say, your destiny has reached its end"

With a lonely expression that bares the soul
I make my way into the valley the minister saw in his dream
Pushing aside the welling clouds and welling sheep

This valley is the "gate of the mysterious woman"
Because it falls into the domain of shadows, it is called the shadowy gate

It has eternally moving lips
And because the water of the netherworld wells within
They are called lips of shadow

Yet there are teeth here as well
Rugged teeth of rock
That tear apart the dead

"*The spirit of the valley does not die*"
"*Empty yet inexhaustible*"
Yet the spirit of the valley does wail
As she gives birth over and over again

The River

    I am on a train. A sleepy rail alongside a mountain. The rails are slightly rusted. Someone is seated next to me. A completely boring man wearing glasses. I don't have anything to say to him so I begin to doze off when suddenly the train clatters to a stop at a country station surrounded by gravestones. Are the people getting off all dead? I begin to doze off again when I realize that the rhythmic clattering and vibrations of the train have grown more pronounced. I raise my eyes and see we are crossing a steel-girdered bridge. A river. That river! I hurriedly get off at the next stop. The man next to me is screaming something through the window, but I just see his mouth moving and cannot hear a sound.

    I go to get out my ticket at the gate, but I realize it is gone. I am anxiously digging through my shoulder bag when the stationmaster comes to me with a slip of paper in hand. He tells me I should write down the name of the station where I got on and the name of this station. I don't know either. With an expression that indicates this is too much work, he tells me it really doesn't matter. I should just write something. In the most indecipherable letters I can muster, I write the letter *aun* in something that looks like Phoenician or Minoan Linear B script, and I hand it over to him with a dramatic gesture. That should be fine, he says. He takes it and files it away.

    When I leave, there is a dog waiting for me. It is Tarō, my dog when I was a little girl; he had disappeared one day and never returned. A mixture of a Sakhalin and a Shiba, he had perfectly triangular little ears that stood on end, a thick frame, and beautiful brown fur with a tinge of gold. The dog approaches and nestles up to my legs as if thinking back over the old days. Tarō! You've been alive all this time?

The mountains have taken on the same golden brown hue as Tarō's fur. Late autumn, is it? The leaves are all bright gold, but as the day starts to draw to a close, damp shadows emerge. I catch the aroma of the river, and I begin to walk in that direction. Tarō follows. Every once in a while, his moist nose lightly brushes the back of my calf. The chilly nose of an animal.

There are autumn bellflowers blooming in a clearing in the woods. Distorted buds of bluish purple. Like scattered blue flames, they bloom at my feet. The fox fires that announce the presence of the supernatural have taken the shape of flowers and are burning in the shade of the taller grass. At some point without my realizing it, Tarō has transformed into a fox. His ears, ordinarily equilateral triangles, have grown into long isosceles triangles. His face has grown long, and his curly tail stretches out straight to the back.

The indications of the coming dusk grow deeper, and the atmosphere takes on a heavy closeness. Each individual particle of air is tinged with a mysterious ghostliness, making the atmosphere flicker with phosphorescent light. Tarō, now transformed into a fox, lets out a howl and runs into the depths of the forest, leaving me with nothing but the sound of the river.

Chewing on a Eucalyptus Leaf

How long has it been since I planted the eucalyptus tree? Twenty years?

Eucalyptuses have round, bluish-green leaves coated with a white, dreamy powder like ground sesame, and their branches bend gracefully, giving the pleasantly scented trees an otherworldly air. Drawn to them for these reasons, I decided to plant a sapling in front of my window, next to the doghouse. I looked forward to opening the window in the mornings and evenings, gazing at its young leaves, and taking a deep, easy breath, filling my lungs with its mentholated aroma.

The sapling grew before my very eyes. In summer, it provided cool shade for the doghouse beneath. Our dog Gorō lived a long life in its shadow and died stretched out at the base of the tree. Two generations later, our third dog, a female Shiba named Asa, was just about in her prime. When she was a puppy, the lovely canopy of the eucalyptus had already spread over the roof of the second story. By the time she reached adulthood, the tree was so huge that if you were to look at it from afar, our home would have looked like a doghouse at its base.

Because eucalyptus trees are evergreen, they do not drop their leaves all at once. If anything, they are more likely to drop them in the spring than in the autumn, but still, they drop a few at a time continually throughout the year. Although I say "a few," the tree has as many leaves as the sky has stars. No sooner would I get done sweeping up the leaves in the garden than I would turn around to find the entire thing once again buried in newly fallen reddish leaves. Even if I swept the garden conscientiously every day, there were so many leaves that I could not possibly stuff them all in garbage bags or plastic trash cans. Before long, I became fed up and abandoned the idea of sweeping altogether. As the years passed, the tree grew more and more quickly, and the number of leaves multiplying on the branches—and therefore the number of falling leaves—rose exponentially. At that rate, the leaves would probably overflow the first floor of the house like rising water in a flood.

My prediction came true even sooner than I had anticipated. One morning in late spring, a squirrel descended to a low branch and nodded to me over and over as if inviting me into his world. I decided to move. I would move into the tree. How much more spacious it would be in that skyscraper of a tree than in my cramped house, which was being buried in leaves before my very eyes!

From the second-story veranda, I leaned a ladder against the trunk of the tree. After starting Asa up the ladder before me, I began climbing. Neither humans nor dogs are too adept at climbing trees. We could never hope for the nimbleness of a squirrel or a monkey. However, once we finally reached the lowest limb, which was still higher than the roof of the second story, I found we could move from limb to limb with surprising ease. The circumference of the lowest limb was twice the width of my arms, and as it traced its gentle curve against the sky, it formed junctions with the neighboring branches like highway interchanges.

Further along, the gigantic bough divided into numerous smaller ones. Obstructing the intersection of the forking paths was a great monkey with eyes like vermilion ground cherries. He stood as still as a statue of a deity guarding the crossroads. Asa was paralyzed by fear, but I scooped her up in my arms, greeted the dignified inhabitant of our eucalyptus tree, and walked by without incident.

Actually, the original inhabitants of the tree seem to be the serpents. When they are perfectly still, you can hardly distinguish them from the branches. The young twigs are whitish green, but there is also a thin variety of snake that is exactly the same color. The big branches look like big snakes, and the thin twigs look like thin ones. I sometimes see serpents slithering along a limb, lifting their heads, and branching into the emptiness like small twigs. I also sometimes see squirrels scurrying fearlessly across a snake stretched like a bridge between two branches.

Although this tree is no more than twenty years old, it has numerous hollows, not just in the trunk itself, but hidden in the larger branches as well. When I found one with a narrow entrance and spacious interior, I decided to use it as my bedroom.

When the wind stirs the eucalyptus leaves, they rub together and release a faint aroma that, together with the gentle sound of rustling, caresses and soothes the spirit. When the day draws to a close, the luxurious canopy of the tree becomes studded with stars, and the wind stirs it ever so gently in its breeze. On nights when the wind is strong, some of the stars flutter to earth together with the leaves. The stars glitter with a pale blue light on the ground for a few moments, but then they turn reddish and dull and disappear without a trace, like cinders fallen from a sparkler.

The first day we climbed into the tree, only a few hours had passed before I felt my breathing grow easy and my body seemed far lighter than ever before. Two or three days later, my body had become more agile, making it much easier to adapt to life in the tree. When I chewed on a eucalyptus leaf, the confusion of the human world seemed so remote and incomprehensible that I felt like I had left it altogether and become a koala. Asa did not seem to undergo any significant changes. Her motor abilities were by nature much more developed than those of a human, so she could run from branch to branch without any trouble at all.

Since I use my arms and legs every day to travel the paths formed by the branches, my movements have grown more and more simian. Even within the course of a single generation, it seems possible to evolve rapidly into an ape. The great monkey who stood in our path the first day and glared at us with his bright orange eyes sometimes adopts a protective attitude toward me. I have become his protégée. On days like yesterday when I am reluctant to jump to a branch that is just out of reach, he will even extend a helping hand from above.

Other than the monkey, serpents, and squirrels, most of the inhabitants of the eucalyptus hide deep in the foliage during the day. Every once in a while, I catch a glimpse of a bushy tail the color of a fawn disappearing into the shade of the branches. Sometimes I see a curved horn peeking out from the leaves. These glimpses are so fleeting that I think my eyes are playing tricks on me. I cannot see what the creatures are or how many there might be. When night falls however, I see one or two pairs of blue or golden eyes twinkling at the entrance of our bedroom, and I know that whoever they are, they are watching over us. They have never once tried to harm us.

One night, one pair of eyes came unusually close, and I heard a faint growl. Judging from the size of the eyes with their sharp glint, I could tell they belonged to a fairly large beast. Still, Asa was not afraid. She pricked her ears and growled back. As the pair of eyes outside retreated, she stepped forward to chase the intruder off. I knew she was in danger, but she did not listen when I commanded her to stop. She bounded into the dense foliage, chasing the creature as it turned its back and fled.

Asa did not return that night. I stayed awake with my ears open, but there was nothing to be heard. Some fleas Asa had left behind bit my thigh and made it swell. The next morning however, she came home as if nothing had happened.

Not even a hundred days have passed since we started our arboreal life, but already the eucalyptus has become more than just a home. It has become our world, our universe. It stretches from earth to the sky, and as it grows, it twists slightly like a living Tower of Babel. Each of the large limbs emerging from the trunk is as grand as a thousand-year-old redwood or a gigantic serpent covered in green moss. In just a few days, even the tiny twigs grow to be as large as the great boughs. Infinite numbers of branches of every size intersect to form complicated patterns. It is as if they are trying to capture as much space as possible in their wide net. This latticework is covered in beautiful silvery leaves that remain throughout the year. As a result, one cannot possibly know more than a hundredth of the network's secrets or see even a tiny fraction of its inhabitants.

Apart from my bedroom, my favorite place in this gigantic mansion is the room I call "the parlor." It consists of a flat place where a limb divides in two. When I first saw it, it was about eighteen square feet, but now it has almost tripled in size. When I lie face up on the bumpy surface of the triangular parlor, the gigantic canopy covering the sky begins to revolve slowly, and I experience a feeling like vertigo. The twisted trunk, the bowed branches... They are an assembly of infinite serpents of all sizes, big and small... The entire tree is like an enormous dragon of plant life, and this dragon has an infinite number of necks that divide endlessly as they stretch toward heaven. The sweeping melody of the wind stroking the gigantic tree echoes pleasantly in my ears. Caught in this green whirlwind, I feel like I am ascending slowly into the heavens. This is not just because of the vertigo. The distance between the ground and me in the treetop is growing constantly.

Looking down, I see that the ladder we used to climb from the veranda into the tree still has not fallen. It stands half-buried in leaves, but the tree has grown so quickly that it has become utterly impossible for us to return home. The house now looks as small as a matchbox. What's more, the entire first story has been buried in leaves. The only thing still visible is the roof of the second story, which looks as if it has been shingled in leaves. There is no trace of the doghouse of course. But none of that matters. We never want to return.

There is only one thing that bothers me. Asa has started howling. She does it every evening. Before when she howled, she would arch her head upward, point her nose to the sky, and let forth a long plaintive cry as if howling at the moon. Now, she lets her head hang low and howls at the ground below. Her belly has swelled until it is quite plump. Clearly, she is carrying a child. No doubt this is the result of that night when she was lured in the darkness by that mysterious pair of eyes. I wonder what this means. Did the eyes belong to an enormous male cur? Or could they have belonged to something else altogether...?

The images of various strange creatures flash through my mind—creatures that are half dog and half wolf or baboon. I picture strangely shaped creatures like centaurs or sphinxes, and then I envision them as indistinct, bloody lumps wriggling inside Asa's uterus. The only way to rid myself of these oppressive thoughts is to chew several round young leaves. Still, the belly of my small Shiba, which hides this unknown and unknowable creature, grows bigger by the day. When night falls, Asa hangs her head and howls at her small house lost below. As I listen to her melancholy voice, I take a breath so deep that the aroma of the stratospheric eucalyptus tree permeates every cell of my body. I am sure our progress into the heavens is more than just a dream, but in those moments, even I feel a nostalgic homesickness for terrestrial life welling within.

FROM *The Land of the Long River* (2000)

River

Like a stake, the river penetrates
Past, present, future

■

This river exists alone in the world
This river cleaves the world in two
Like an authoritative injunction
Impartially dividing
The living on the east bank
And the dead on the west

■

—Our craft has started its preparations to land
Will it land on the east bank
Or on the west?
—Whichever it may be, fasten your seat belt tight

Flow

Moving
Unmoving

Unmoving
Moving

The river presses the dense mass of water forward
And flows into eternity

Boat

On the west bank live the dead
And on the east bank the living

Traveling between them
Is this boat

Whither has the stone god gone—he who once stood
In the flow and who left only his right foot behind?

Tethered to the ankle as large as a man's arms are wide
Is this boat

Whither has the lame god wandered? The boatmen beneath
Give no thought to the whereabouts of the gods

Netherworld

Murdered
Torn limb from limb
The god was scattered across the earth

In a papyrus boat painted with pitch
The goddess weeps as she collects the pieces
(The river is a river of tears)
She connects the fragments of flesh
And intones great incantations

And as she chants, his wounds heal
And as she chants, his eyes open

—But what is this, my beloved husband?
Though thou hast come back, come to life once again
Thou shalt return from the netherworld nevermore

Entertainment

Once a year
The god travels down the river aboard a boat
To meet the goddess

Oh blessed divinity, amuse thyself
For amusement is what best befits the gods

We shall hold papyrus flowers on high
And pass through the facing rows of
Crouching ram-shaped gods who protect us

We shall descend to the temple dock
To see the god on his sacred way

Oh, how flat the corners
Of our eyes are as we extend our gaze
So far, so very far
Over the smooth surface of the water!

Dawn

Stretching her supple body
The goddess forms a lofty arc over the earth

Stars scattered over her azure body
Like fine flecks of gold in lapis lazuli

Nut, the living vault of heaven
Gives birth to the sun each morning

And with the blood of her holy delivery
She dyes the eastern sky deep, deep red

Letter

On a sandy road lined with meager patches of grass
A boy leads an ox
An emaciated ox
With a prominently protruding spine

The ox's face does not protrude from the ox's face
What protrudes are two horns
Since ancient times generations of oxen have had the face of oxen
And from that face mankind made its first letter
Awa
Aleph
Alpha

For millennia, oxen have remained unchanged
When handled by men, their heads are turned both up and down
Awa
Aleph
Alpha   Aaaa—
Humming this song
The thin boy pulls the thin bull
Along the sandy road lined with meager patches of grass

FROM *A Souvenir of Wind:* Haiku (2003)

the rain of the
meteor shower in Leo
lets up on the cancer ward

獅子座流星雨果てて蟹座の病棟へ

the death
inside my body
is a soft winter wart

身の内に死はやはらかき冬の疣

when a cat in heat passes
the security light
switches on

戀猫の通ればともる防犯灯

as the bandages are undone
I find myself
a springtime mummy

繃帯をほどけば春のミイラかな

swim on, old woman!
fallen cherry petals float
on the Milky Way

嫗泳げよ花屑浮かぶ天の川

here too
in a remote region
I bend my knees and pick bracken

膝曲げてここも邊土の蕨摘み

so fresh
the pattern after sweeping
the summer sumō ring

夏土俵掃く箒目のあたらしき

yesterday, today, tomorrow
they are all a white field
in summer

昨日今日明日(あした)も白き夏野かな

the young leaves
all the shapes of hearts
the shapes of eyes

若葉みな心臓のかたち眼のかたち

even the gecko
by the window each morning
on such close terms!

朝朝の窓の守宮(やもり)も親しさよ

how round
the fingers of the gecko
on the other side of the glass

玻璃ごしや守宮のゆびのまろきこと

I turn back to look
and in my face
such wild abandon and pallor

うつむけば顔に婆娑羅と青薄

   In memory of Yagawa Sumiko

traces of you
grow still beneath
a myriad of green leaves

萬緑の底に面影鎮もりぬ

may the water of
these short summer nights grow clear
the river of forgetfulness

短夜の水澄みてあれ忘れ川

dead souls—
the hydrangeas
lose their color so easily

魂魄やあぢさゐは色褪せやすき

the galingale—
my parents' home
so long after losing them

蚊帳吊草や失せて久しき父母の家

the linen clothes and Panama hat
my father had
so long ago

むかし父ありき麻服パナマ帽

my mother's arms
rolling up the reed blinds
were so white, so long ago

むかし母すだれ巻き上ぐる腕白し

having completely forgotten
my head is light—
the rattan pillow

忘れ盡して輕き頭や籠枕

the garden is
full of discarded cicada shells
full of holes

庭は蝉の脱殻だらけ穴だらけ

dozing gently
with book in hand
the call of cicadas like a rain shower

本を手に居眠るやすしせみしぐれ

In ancient China there was a custom of placing jade cicadas in the mouths of corpses

holding a jade cicada
how I want to listen to the cicadas
calling out like a summer shower

玉蝉（ぎょくせん）を含み聽かばやせみしぐれ

the whereabouts of the wind
as it transfers
riding the grass

草の背を乗りつぐ風の行方かな

FROM *Upon Breaking the Seal* (2004)

After Half a Century

Finally after half a century, a clearly observable law has been found:
For mankind, all matters proceed
Along geometric lines

(If you put one grain of rice on the first intersection of a game board, two grains of rice on the second, four grains of rice on the third, and continue along these lines, what vast quantities will you have by the time the board is covered? When the ancient king was told the answer, how surprised he was . . .)

By the time I realized what was happening, I was clinging to the earth
So I would not be shaken off as it spun with ever greater speed
My hair, dyed in two parts with night and day, had come loose
(Yet still I toyed with dice in one hand)

As it turns, it is stripped page by page like a calendar pad growing thin
A cabbage growing small, shorn of leaves before our eyes
Once, this planet had plenty of moisture
(But that was in the days when those things that now belong to dead languages—
Things such as *dawn, looks,* and *smiles*—were still portents of things to come)
That's right, for mankind, all matters proceed along geometric lines

Four and a half more centuries into the future
The shriveled brain that revolves

Rattling in the cranium's hollow will grow still
Like the pale eye of a hurricane

All will see its resolution in those moments
As the rolling dice tumble, turning up their black eyes
Then finally coming to a halt

The Piece of Mail, or My Nightmare

If I break the seal, something terrible will happen
Still I cannot throw it away
So the envelope sits, seal unbroken
On my desk for weeks

With seal unbroken, the envelope
Gradually grows thicker and thicker
The message grows more complicated
The terrible thing grows worse and worse
Calling for emergency measures

I know who sent it
That is why I do not want to read it
If I read it, something terrible will happen
Still I cannot throw it away
I cannot toss it into the fire
If I do, it might explode

What shall I do? What shall I do?

The sealed envelope
Swollen as if ready to give birth
Squirms upon the desktop

Fish

Sit properly, legs folded, before your tray
And pluck at the jellied fish upon your plate
The unshakable order of the fish will reveal itself
The ordered knots of the backbone connecting head to tail

From each joint of the vertebrae
Parallel lines radiate at equidistant intervals
Cold, white, and sharp
Disobeying both tongue and utensil

The skeletal structure that remains
Is the substance of the fish, the essence
(The essence being, in other words, its corpse)

Then, with eyes gouged out, it slides off the plate
And is tossed into darkness
As if unclean

Cultivation

My aunt who has descended from the mountains
Lines up flower pots on the shelf
Cultivating the heads of infants, still small and fragile

*—Look, green sprouts are peeping out
  From the slits beneath the eyelids*

Each morning, she uses the watering can
To sprinkle them with lukewarm milk and thin rice gruel
And sometimes things so hot they scald

*—I wonder what kind of flowers
  Will appear in each pot
  I can hardly wait . . .*

She smiles contentedly to herself

Twice Round the Loop Line

Chance Meeting

A high-pitched roar from the opposite direction
I pass by you as you approach
And nod at your passing form

(*Was that really you?*)

A momentary recognition
Afterward, the Doppler effect
A fading, tapering wail
Until we meet again

But how many centuries will pass
Before I meet you again (accompanied by that roar)—
You with your face utterly changed?

Pilgrimage

Even if the sun is setting as I pass Nippori
I will not try to disembark
This is a seated pilgrimage
Leisurely
I go round in circles
From one place name to the next
A necklace of stations strung together
As I finger my rosary
I travel round the eternal loop line
A humble seeker of the way
Moving from one sacred place to the next

Turning the Wheel of Transmigration
On the painting of throwing oneself to the tiger

Right before the starving tiger who comes with cub in tow
The young man falls
He falls from the cliff to the tigers below

By saving the starving tigers, mother and child
The prince of deep compassion will become the Buddha
Deep within the belly of the beast

But by ingesting and digesting the Buddha
What part of the tigers themselves
Will become the Buddha too?

When the rescued cub grows
And has cubs of its own
Will another young man fall from a cliff for them as well?

> *(Oh, great packs of tigers flood the world*
> *Dividing the earth into black and gold, darkness and light!)*

Was the bodhisattva's sacrifice a deed that ends in a single act
Or does the Buddha pass through the endlessly turning wheel of transmigration
Each time he is passed from the jaws of one tiger to another?

Garden of Paradise

As the fruit upon the fig tree swells
The faint aroma of paradise lost returns
Insects gather round—
Crawling insects, flying insects, walking insects of all sorts

Ants crawl inside through the hole
In the swollen, reddish purple buttocks
Next the beetles crawl inside
Never to come out again

I am human so I hold back
It is still a little firm
Tomorrow or the next day, it will be just right
But the next day, its side has been hollowed out

What quick-eyed bulbuls, so early to rise!
What sharp, accurate beaks!

In the deep, gaping wound
The despairing scent of paradise rises

Unable to wait, I crawl inside after the beetles
I who gazed at the fig from the outside
Eat away at the fig from within
Isn't this remarkably amusing?

No, this is the garden of paradise
As I digest the fig
I am digested by it
And lose my human form once again

Summer Letter

A letter will come from the day after tomorrow
In it, tomorrow's events will be recorded
By tomorrow, I mean yesterday
Will my tomorrow self be well or not?

Tomorrow and yesterday face one another
With today as a turning point
Everyone misreads them
Mistaking tomorrow for yesterday
And yesterday for tomorrow

The cicadas will bore many holes in the ground
Crawl out and begin to buzz
But will that be tomorrow or yesterday?
My head spins round and round

I face backward
I face forward
Unwilling to pass into tomorrow
I try to move forward but just fall behind

Cicadas cluster on the trees
And chirp incessantly

And that is how summer goes by
Summer and autumn facing one another
With today as a turning point

Look! A letter has come from the day before yesterday
The day before yesterday was autumn
The day after tomorrow is summer
As I let empty cicada shells settle in my hair
Was my yesterday self well or not?
Was my yesterday self
Well or not?

FROM *Person of the Playful Star:* Tanka (2005)

wondering
to what family
the sycamore belongs
I open the plant guide—
the sycamore family

鈴懸は何科ならむと植物の図鑑開けばスズカケノキ科

summer passes—
the used book
Hecate and Dog
encountered while walking
the university streets

夏過ぎし大学街をあゆみゐて会いたる古書「ヘカーテと犬」

to the corner park
where I read my book
Hecate and Dog
an old woman approaches
black dog in tow

「ヘカーテと犬」読みいたる辻公園老女来たれり黒き犬連れ

the Arab youth
speaks on and on
the bubbles of his
consonants growing
in number upon his lips

唇に子音の泡をふやしつつ語りてやまぬアラブ青年

although
the meaning is unclear
I still take pleasure
in the rustling, rising waves
of consonants and vowels

意味不明ながらたのしむさわさわと子音母音の波のたかまり

the palm of the hand
has both back and front
turning it over and back again
a day spent in sickness
draws to a close

てのひらに裏表あり裏返し表返して病める日暮れぬ

the faint wind of the body
dislodges and blows
smoothly on its way
half the body is sea
half the body mountain

身のあはひ風するすると抜けてゆく半身は海半身は山

The Rostropovich recital

in the grand hall
he made the strings quiver
and rise in waves
all alone, the old man
amused himself with his cello

大ホールに弦をそよがせ波うたせ翁はひとりチェロと遊べり

the unaccompanied cello
illuminated in a small spotlight
the old man
upon the stage
utterly alone

無伴奏のチェロは小さく照らされて舞台にまことひとりの翁

surrounded by my
thousands of tomes
will I grow old
never knowing the art
of deciphering the heavens?

星空を読み解^{すべ}術も知らずして老ゆか萬巻の書に囲まれて

I listen to songs
of someone handsome
at the apex of night
the Milky Way overflows
the stars boil over and fall

佳きひとの偲び歌聴く夜の極み銀河あふれて星たぎり落つ

a male mantis
quietly consumed
by the female
the navy blue of the gentian flower
grows swiftly dark with twilight

雄かまきりおとなしく雌に喰はれてゐて龍膽の紺にはかに昏るる

a short summer night
I wake as the flowers
seem to shrivel completely away
beside the pillow that I,
the dead woman, use

死者われの枕辺の花ことごとくしぼむとみえて覚めし短夜

there is a hole at
the end of night
a secret
surrounded by red
road construction lamps

夜の果に穴あり道路工事中赤きランプの囲める秘密

the drowning victim
spreads her hair wide
facing downward
opening her eyes to the bottom
of the nighttime water

水死者は黒髪ひろげうつ伏せに夜の水底にまなこひらける

as we move forward
rocked between
dream and reality
intermittent lines of gravestones
along the train tracks

ゆめうつつ揺られてゆけば沿線は点点として墓石つらなる

dreams of travel or
perhaps travel in a dream
I make my connections
rocked back and forth
sleeping and waking in turns

旅の夢はた夢の旅ゆられつつさめつねむりつ乗り継いでゆく

Mother passes on

already reflecting
nothing of this world
her retinas open wide
and she sinks in the darkness
of the netherworld

もはや世に映すものなき網膜をひろげて黄泉の闇に沈めむ

we place flowers upon
her pale, cold
forehead
then cover
the icebox-like coffin

青白く冷えにし額に花を置き氷庫の如き棺に蓋す

in the morning breeze
the window of the wake room
now stands open
summer has come
over the body of the deceased

朝風にいま開け放す通夜の窓屍の上に夏立ちにけり

there are dead who
mingle with the north wind
soar through the empty sky
raise their voices and
sing in falsetto

北風にまぎれ虚空を翔りつつ裏声あげて歌ふ死者あり

old but still alive
father grows ill
his shadow has grown thin
but his hairy eyebrows are
still white and thick

老残の父病みて影うすくあれど太き眉毛は白きまま濃し

several volumes of
classical Chinese poetry
come from father
who can no longer read
as autumn grows deep

父もはや文字が読めずと送り来ぬ漢詩数巻秋深むころ

On hearing of the Shōwa Emperor's critical condition

because he spilled
the blood of tens of thousands
he receives
big blood transfusions
and cannot die

幾萬人に血を流させし人なれば大量の輸血受けて死なれず

after sixty years of walking
my shadow lies
exhausted
where it falls
and doesn't try to get up

六十年歩み疲れてわが影の地に倒れ伏し起きむとはせず

karma of women
karma of men
entangling and
dying the world the pattern
of a serpent's stomach

女の業男の業と絡み合ひ蛇腹模様に世を染めなせり

like a twisted rope
the karma of men and women
continually clinging
continually drawn
to one another

あざなへる縄にも似たる女男の業互みに縋り曳きずられつつ

in the earth
countless corpses
form layers and
raise their voices
as they writhe incessantly

大地には無数の死者が層をなし声こもらせてうごめきやまぬ

still leaning
the wooden marker
over the high-ranking
infantryman's grave
wet with freezing rain

陸軍歩兵上等兵の木の墓標かたむきしまま氷雨に濡るる

a shower on
the taut nude form
one part of
the young man's flesh
heavily bears fruit

締りたる裸形にシャワー少年の肉ひとところ重くみのれる

of the nine holes of
the human body
seven are concentrated in the face—
how terrifying
the eyes, nose, ears, and mouth

身の九竅七つまで顔にあつまれり　げにおそろしきや目鼻耳口

I try to go back to my hometown
where wisteria hung
in the pale light of dawn
but no longer
do I know the way home

薄明の藤花垂るるふるさとへ帰らむとすれど道の知らなく

transparent, the wind
passes through my palms held high
turning my life's pages
leaving it thinner and thinner
before my very eyes

かざす掌(て)に風は透けたりわが生涯(ひとよ)みるみるうすくめくれゆくかな

drawing shadows
drawing gazes
I wander confused
a single sick body in
a spacious field of flowers

影曳きてまなざし曳きて行きまどふ病める身ひとつ広き花野に

The meteor shower in Leo, November 2001

for this last look
I've wrapped my body
in a thick gown and come
outside to meet the
clusters of falling stars

見をさめと厚きガウンに身をつつみ流星の群れに遭ひにいでたり

Among the constellations is the crab called Cancer, the same name as the disease

I bathe
to my heart's content
in the meteor shower
later in the cancer ward
I bathe in radiation

流星雨心ゆくまで浴びてのち癌病棟に放射線浴ぶ

my diagnosis
of cancer was a notice
of pregnancy too
consecrated in the shrine of children
is the god of cancer

癌告知は受胎告知にてありしかなわが「子の宮」に癌を祀りて

my flesh
cut crosswise
to form round slices
tens of tomograms
lined up in a row

にくたいは輪切りにされて並べらる幾十枚の断層写真

if I were a tree
cutting me crosswise would
produce beautiful rings
but cutting my body just shows
an overgrown thicket

樹木ならば美しき年輪顕はれむわが身の輪切りただおどろなる

one cannot read
the rings of a tree in
these cross sections of flesh—
the endpoint of a disease
of dubious distinction

にくたいの輪切りに年輪よみとれずあやめあやしき病ひゆくすゑ

accustomed to living
in a storehouse of grasses
I have seen
the leaves of language
flourish and wither away

草の府に住みならはして言の葉の繁れるを見き枯れゆくを見き

various kinds
of wonders
have lost their wonder
wonderland is headed
for its own destruction

さまざまのふしぎがふしぎでなくなりて不思議の国は滅びに向かふ

In Italy, on seeing the statues of Hadrian and Antinous in the same room

face to face
with his beloved
the emperor has turned to stone
in a museum
in the old capital

皇帝はその寵童と向き合ひて石と化したり古都の博物館(ムーセオ)

did he give bread
even to the slaves?
carved in stone
the Roman emperor
crowned with a halo of barley

奴隷にもパン与へしや石彫の麦の穂冠のローマ皇帝

On the cathedral of bones

what do they
intend to burn
piling these desiccated bones
high like firewood
as if to say *memento mori*?

枯骨を薪のごとくに積みかさね何燃やさむか「死を想へ」とて

On seeing the mosaic of the creation of Adam in San Marco Basilica, Venice

with the fig leaf
he should cover his chest
and hide the scar
where God took
his rib away

無花果の葉をもて胸は覆ふべし神の取りたる肋骨のあと

the holy child
is always at the breast
of the holy mother
so why not call
the holy mother God?

御子はつねに御母の胸に在するをなにとて聖母を神とは呼ばぬ

Mayan ruins

a great iguana
dozing on the stone ruins
is he gazing at
the dreams of
a thousand years?

大イグアナ遺跡の石に居眠れり千年の夢みつつあらむか

the sun
over Mayan lands
has grown ancient
its rays desiccate
fiercely empty

マヤ族の地に太陽は古びたり日差_{かわ}燥きて激しく虚し

I who roll the dice
and play the game
am a person of the playful star
rolling through
the forbidden heavens

骰子_{さい}振つて遊べるわれや禁断の天を転がる遊星の人

born onto
this playful star
of deep green
why don't we dedicate ourselves
to playing for all we are worth?

みどり濃きこの遊星に生まれてきてなどひたすらに遊ばざらめや

the gods give birth to
people on this planet
a confused and wandering star
where heaven moves
and earth moves

神神は天動地動戸惑へるこの惑星に人生みつけぬ

Translator's Notes

WITHERED FIELD

The use of metaphor in this poem echoes that of the final, famous poem by the seventeenth-century haiku poet Matsuo Bashō: "Ill on a journey / Dreams race round and round / On the withered field." Drawing upon the metaphor of a withered field (*kareno*) in winter as the site where life's dreams and dramas are played out, Tada created this poem about walking across the boundless field of life, weathering hardships.

UNIVERSE OF THE ROSE

In *Teihon Tada Chimako shishū* [*The Authoritative Edition of the Poetry of Tada Chimako*], published in 1994, Tada wrote, "The words in roman letters included as a headnote for the 'Universe of the Rose' are the scientific name for LSD and hint at my experiences taking the drug. There is also an epigraph from Nicholas of Cusa, but looking for this passage in his works would be wasted effort. The reason is that I, as the author, have simply taken on this philosopher's name in order to create a quote for my own poem; however, it would not be unnatural to imagine that a thinker working with the idea of *coincidentia oppositorum* (the coincidence of opposites) might have said something like this" (p. 605).

THE TOWN OF MIRRORS, OR FOREST OF EYES

In this work, Tada brings together a series of seemingly separate poems that, like a musical set of theme and variations, deals with seeing and being seen. Abashiri, which appears in the first section, is written with the characters meaning "net" and "running" (網走) and is a city in northeastern Hokkaidō, the northernmost of the major islands of Japan. Habomai, written with the characters meaning "teeth" and "dance" (歯舞), is a small archipelago off Hokkaidō. In this section, Tada uses these images to evoke distant places, while at the same time playing with the literal meaning of the names. Toward the end of the first section, Tada makes a reference to *Oku no hosomichi* [*Narrow Road to a Far Province*], the famous travel journal

135

by Bashō, in which he describes his two-and-a-half-year journey to the northern reaches of Japan.

In the third section, Tada refers to the plight of men who desire erotic contact with other men and cruise restrooms and other public areas while trying to avoid the surveillance of authorities. Over the years, Tada had a number of close, openly gay friends, including the poets Aizawa Keizō and Takahashi Mutsuo, both of whom wrote a great deal of poetry in the late 1960s and 1970s about their experiences and the culture of homoerotic desire.

In the fourth section, Tada uses the image of a woman cooking her own eyes. In Japanese, an egg fried sunny side up is called a "fried eye" (*medama-yaki*) because of the appearance of the yolk surrounded by the cornea-like egg white.

GRAVE OF HYACINTH

In Greek myth, Hyacinth (also called Hyacinthus), the beloved of Apollo, was accidentally killed when a discus struck him in the head. Rather than allowing the underworld to claim him, Apollo used Hyacinth's blood to create the flower that bears his name.

THE WELL

In the eighth and ninth lines, Tada plays with the sound of the plant name "chaff-flower" (*inokozuchi*), which in Japanese resembles the word for "life force" (*inochi*).

THE HOUSEMATE

In Japanese, the game peek-a-boo is called *inai-inai-baa*. The word *inai* means "is not present" or "does not exist." *Baa* is the word used when someone suddenly reveals themselves, but it also sounds like the word meaning "old lady." The translation "old peek-a-boo granny who was not there" is an attempt to convey both meanings. In the section in which the old lady and the narrator are talking about the narrator's son, the old lady makes a clever play on the double meaning of *motte iru mono* (meaning both "things one has" and "because it's attractive") in her statement *Watashi no motte inai mono bakari motte iru mono* (translated here as "Because the things that attract me are the things I don't have"). Later in the same section, the old lady makes a pun on the fact that the first character in the word meaning "old age" (*rōkyō*) is a homonym for the character meaning "wolf."

GARDEN OF ABSENCE

The word "mirage" is written with the characters meaning "clam air towers" (*shinkirō* 蜃気楼), a reference to Chinese folktales of clams that could produce illusory underwater buildings with their bubbles. Tada uses the word to describe a mirage in an imaginary lake, thus evoking these resonances.

DESTINY OF PATHS

Eratosthenes of Cyrene (276–194 BCE) was a mathematician and geographer who devised the system of latitude and longitude and calculated the circumference of the earth. *Liezi* is the name of a text compiled around the fourth century BCE and attributed largely to the philosopher Lie Yukou. The real source of the classical Chinese phrase to which Tada refers is the *Shuolin xun* [*Discourse on Forests*] in *Huainanzi* [*Masters of Huainan*], from the second century BCE. Many of the surviving thoughts of the fourth-century BCE philosopher Yang Zhu are recorded in chapter 7 of the *Liezi*. This is the source of the story about the sheep that Tada mentions in this poem. In it, Yang Zhu uses the story of his neighbor to discuss the idea that there are many paths from a single point of departure, and even people who start on similar philosophical paths will eventually diverge.

FROM *A SPRAY OF WATER*: TANKA

There is a great deal of debate about the way that tanka and haiku might best be translated into English, since both typically consist of a single metered line of Japanese text. The prominent translator Hiroaki Sato has advocated a one-line approach, arguing that the concept of lineation is not part of traditional Japanese poetics. In his opinion, to break a translation into multiple lines discards the visual smoothness of the single line of the original and gives a false impression of the way the poem functions. While Sato's approach is not without reason, I have followed the more common tendency among English translators to break tanka and haiku into multiple lines in order to give a sense of the internal rhythm of the poem. I have rendered tanka in five lines, hoping to approximate the internal structure of 5–7–5–7–7 morae; similarly, I have rendered haiku in three lines to hint at the internal structure of 5–7–5 morae. It is also worth noting that Japanese words tend to have more syllables than English words, so English translations typically consist of fewer syllables than one would find in the metric pattern of the Japanese. Any attempt to render the exact metrical pattern of the original would require "padding"—extra words to fill out the syllabic count. This, plus the fact that English speakers are not trained like the Japanese to hear patterns of five and seven syllables, has led me not to attempt to replicate the exact metric patterns of the Japanese.

"in the pale light of / stringed music / the river trembles / a fine filigreed ornament / then flows toward awakening": The word *yōraku,* here translated as "fine filigreed ornament," refers to the kind of finely detailed metal necklaces, headbands, and armbands worn by ancient Indian royalty, as well as the similar adornments placed on Buddhist statues.

LOTOPHAGI

In Greek myth, the Lotophagi (literally "lotus-eaters") were a race of people who lived on an island off North Africa and habitually ate the seeds of a particular kind of lotus that would send them into a narcotic, apathetic sleep.

THE LOST KINGDOM

The author of *Kioku no sho* [*Book of Memories*] was Tada's friend the poet Washisu Shigeo. *Sōmen,* mentioned in the first stanza of the second section, are a kind of thin, white noodle generally eaten cold. The bodhisattva Akasagarbha (Kokūzō in Japanese) mentioned in the same stanza is an enlightened being worshipped in esoteric Buddhism as possessing a degree of wisdom and compassion as vast as the emptiness of the universe. His name in Japanese literally means "store of emptiness."

THE BODHISATTVA'S SEA

In Mahayana Buddhism, a bodhisattva is a transcendent being who delays his or her own enlightenment in order to help the many sentient beings that remain on earth. The bodhisattva Avalokiteshvara (Kannon in Japanese) represents the embodiment of infinite mercy and is sometimes portrayed as having a thousand hands in order to reach out to all creatures on earth. The various numbers in the bodhisattva's speech (*laksa, kioti, ayuta,* etc.) are enormous numbers used in cosmological calculations by the people of ancient India. The wheel of samsara refers to the continually turning cycle of birth, misery, death, and rebirth.

SETTING SUN

An Asura (*ashura* in Japanese) is a powerful being that inhabits one of the Six Realms of Existence described in Mahayana Buddhist cosmology. In Buddhist legends, they are often proud, arrogant, and sometimes even demonic. The kind of stone stupa that Tada describes at the end of the poem is known as a *gorintō* in Japanese, and starting in the Kamakura period (1192–1333), it became a common type of gravestone.

DARK SEA

The character Tada uses in the third stanza for what I have translated as "emptiness" (*kū*) can also mean "sky" (*sora*). The image of the hole in the trap leads to an association with the sky, which leads to another association between starfish and stars. In the beginning of the fourth stanza, Tada's poem contains a double entendre on a word that could mean "no starfish" (*hitode nashi*) or "cruelty, monstrousness" (*hitodenashi*). Moreover, the sound of the word *hitodenashi* echoes the words "of its own accord" (*hitorideni*) in the last line of the previous stanza.

PEACH BLOSSOM SPRING

In the classical Chinese story *Taohuayuan ji* [*Peach Blossom Spring*], the poet Tao Qian, also known as Tao Yuanming (365–427 CE), tells the story of a fisherman who happens upon an orchard of peach trees along a stream. Following the stream and passing through a cave, he comes to a utopian village entirely cut off from the contemporary world. All subsequent attempts by the fisherman and other people to find it again are unsuccessful. As mentioned in the introduction to this book, Tada sometimes compared the place she stayed in Shiga as a fifteen-year-old in 1945 to the Peach Blossom Spring in this Chinese classic.

The language that Tada has chosen in the opening (*Ton'eru o nukereba bosan de aru*) and the beginning of the third stanza (*Toneru o nukereba mono no yo de aru*) echoes the first line of the novel *Yukiguni* [*Snow Country*] by the novelist Kawabata Yasunari (1899–1972): "Coming out of the long tunnel at the provincial border, there was the snow country" (*Kokkyō no nagai ton'eru o nukeru to yukiguni de atta*). The word *bosan* in Tada's opening means "mountains at twilight," but it is written with the characters meaning "gravestone" and "mountain" (墓山). In order to capture the somber feeling of this choice of words, my translation introduces a simile not present in the original: "grave-like mountains at twilight." In the final stanza, Tada mentions the "yellow springs" (*yomi*), the waters that flow through the realm where the ancient Japanese believed the soul went after death.

YAMANBA

In Japanese folklore, the *yamanba* (or *yamauba*) is an old, ghoulish woman who lives in the depths of the mountains and practices magic. According to legend, she assumes the form of an old woman as long as she wears a magical cloak called an *ubakawa,* but when she removes it, she can transform into other shapes, including that of a young woman.

The first and fifth passages contain a reference to the second chapter of *Hokekyō* [*The Lotus Sutra*]. There one finds a statement that even little children who innocently create small stupas out of sand for the Buddha can achieve enlightenment. In the third stanza, Tada states the *yamanba* picks a *hiyu*. She uses the characters that mean "metaphor" or "simile" (比喩), but there is another word with the same pronunciation that means an amaranth flower (莧). In the translation, I have taken the liberty of including both possible meanings.

In the final stanza, Tada mentions a cicada shell. This is a common metaphor in classical Japanese poetry for a transient existence, since the word *utsusemi,* meaning an "empty cicada shell" (空蝉), is a homonym for a word that means "the present body" or "this mortal body" (現身).

THE WOMAN IN THE GARDEN

This poem was inspired by a garden statue of the Madonna. In fact, in a note to *Teihon Tada Chimako shishū* [*The Authoritative Edition of the Poetry of Tada Chimako*], Tada mentions that the French *la jardinière* (the lady of the garden) is a name sometimes used to refer to the Madonna. One sees this in the title of the painting *La belle jardinière,* painted by Raphael and now in the Louvre.

FAVA BEANS

It is said that Pythagoras forbade people to eat fava beans, and although many theories have been advanced to explain why, the reason is not clearly understood. In the next-to-last stanza, Tada compares the swollen beans to Otafuku, a female character in folk dramas who has large swollen cheeks and appears in various popular forms of puppetry and masquerades.

THE TOWN OF ABSENCE

Toward the middle of the poem, Tada refers to a story from Japanese folklore popularly known as "Kobu-tori jiisan" ["The Old Man Who Had His Lump Removed"], about an old man with a large growth hanging off the side of his chin. The lump is taken away by demons who enjoy his dancing and want to keep the lump as collateral to ensure he returns to perform for them again.

FROM DRAGON TEETH SOWN IN THE EARTH

Tada is referring in this poem to the Greek story of Cadmus, who followed the instructions of Athena and threw a dragon's teeth on the soil, thus producing a fierce army of warriors.

FROM THE WINDOWS OF A JOURNEY

The Snail

Among the Mayan ruins at Chichén Itzá on the Yucatán peninsula is a building known as "El Caracol" (the snail) because of a spiraling stone staircase inside. As Tada notes in the poem, the building was used as an astronomical observatory to track celestial events. The Mayan calendar was a complicated system of interlocking cycles of various lengths that could account for both short and extremely long periods of time.

Cigars

In ancient Mexican mythology, Tezcatlipoca was a deity associated with many things, including the night, the north, and obsidian. His name literally means "Smoking Mirror." Tezcatlipoca was important to the Aztecs and Olmecs as well as the Mayans.

Salt

The word in Japanese for cowry shell is *koyasugai* (子安貝), which literally means "child-easing shell," hence the association between the number of shells and the number of children the man would like to have.

Alcohol

The traditional Mayan mathematical system and calendar were both based on a system of twenty numbers. In the Mayan calendar, one of the most basic cycles consists of twenty days. In Japanese, a century plant is called *ryūzetsuran* (龍舌蘭), or literally "a dragon-tongue orchid." This word, which appears in the second stanza, sets up the association with the "fire-dragon" that appears later in the second stanza and in the final line of the poem.

The Snake

The image of a face emerging from the jaws of a snake is a common motif in Mayan art, and it appears on the side of the building known as the "Casa de las monjas" (nunnery) at Uxmal in the Yucatán.

The Couple

According to Aztec history, the ruler Quetzalcoatl founded a city at Chichén Itzá in the year known by the Mayan calendar as One Reed. He then departed to the east, vowing that he would return when the year One Reed recurred in the cyclical calendar. Legend states that when Hernán Cortés arrived in Mexico, it was once again the year of One Reed, and he used the Quetzalcoatl myth to help conquer Montezuma and his people.

REVISITING THE PEACH BLOSSOM SPRING

Like the earlier "Peach Blossom Spring," this poem alludes to the perfect community described in Tao Qian's classical Chinese tale. Tada also alludes to the folktale of Momotarō, the "Peach Boy" who was born out of a peach found floating in a river. For the old couple who had been eager to have a child, Momotarō's discovery brought a new lease on life. Tada remarks in her essay "Jū-go-sai no tōgenkyō" ["The Peach Blossom Spring at Age Fifteen"] that one summer, thirty years after the end of World War II, she took her family to visit the place where she had spent the final months of the war. She had fondly remembered the local temple and the taste of the fish from the river, and she was disappointed to find that the temple had been turned into a vulgar tourist trap and a dam had been built upriver, destroying the fishing. Time had taken revenge on her. This poem was inspired by that visit.

THE MYSTERIOUS WOMAN OF THE SHADOWS,
OR THE VALLEY OF SHEEP

"Mysterious woman of the shadows" is a rough translation of the Chinese word *xuanpin* (玄牝), which appears in the ancient Chinese classic *Dao de jing*. In chapter 6, the *Dao de jing* states, "The spirit of the valley does not die / It is the mysterious woman / The gate of the mysterious woman / Is the root of heaven and earth /

It is continuous yet faint / Use it without forcing it." The exact meaning of this passage is subject to debate, but Tada interprets the "mysterious woman" as the motherly force that represents the origin of life. This leads her to imagine the valley as a vaginal crevice, which smells of amniotic fluid. In Japanese, the word meaning amniotic fluid is *yōsui,* written with two characters meaning "sheep" and "water" (羊水). This leads to an association with the story of sheep that begins in the second stanza. In the collection *Kawa no hotori ni* [*Alongside the Riverbank*], Tada notes that the story of Li Gong is from the classical Chinese work *Xuanshizhi,* a collection of strange stories from the ninth century CE.

In the sixth stanza, Tada mentions the "domain of shadows" (*inpu* or *yomi,* 陰府), a poetic Chinese phrase referring to the realm of the dead. Tada then associates this with "shadowy gate" (*inmon* 陰門), which refers to the vagina. Likewise, she links lips holding back the "water of the netherworld" (*yomi no mizu*) with the vaginal lips (*inshin* 陰唇, literally "shadowy lips"). In Taoist yin-yang cosmology, shadows were associated with yin (陰), the principle tied to the feminine. In this poem, Tada engages in a complicated interlocking series of word associations that forge a close connection between the feminine and shadowy darkness, even death.

In the final stanza, she troubles the all-too-frequent assumption that women represent the source of procreative fertility. The ability to produce is, in a sense, predicated on a sort of death—the death of mothers as individuals. The bodily organs praised as life giving also represent a source of the woman's own death. In the final stanza, Tada quotes two passages from the *Dao de jing,* but then protests the overly simplistic idea of women as happy, eternally giving mothers.

THE RIVER

In Japanese folklore, foxes were shape-shifters that often appeared in different guises and tried to trick human beings. "Fox fires" were floating balls of flame that appeared in the presence of the supernatural.

RIVER

For much of her adult life Tada was fascinated with ancient Egyptian mythology. "River," about the Nile, is the first of a series of poems in the collection *Nagai kawa no aru kuni* [*The Land of the Long River*] inspired by her travels, both real and imaginary, in Egypt. (Tada journeyed to Egypt in 1980.) Each of the poems in this collection has an elegantly simple title of a single kanji character.

NETHERWORLD

This poem refers to the myth of Osiris, killed and dismembered by his evil brother Seth. His loving wife Isis collected his body parts and reassembled them, bandaging them so that he became the first mummy. Despite his wife's loving attention,

Osiris was not able to come back to earth and instead became ruler of the realm of the dead.

DAWN

In ancient Egyptian mythology, Nut is the goddess of the sky who stretches her body, covered with golden stars, over the earth below. Each evening she swallows the sun in the west. The sun passes through her body during the night and in the morning emerges in the east from her vagina. A particularly famous depiction of Nut stretched across the sky appears in the tomb of Ramses V and Ramses VI in the Valley of the Kings, which Tada visited.

FROM *A SOUVENIR OF WIND:* HAIKU

Tada's friend Takahashi Mutsuo collected her unpublished haiku after her death and distributed them at her funeral in this small collection. It was republished as a supplement to *Fū o kiru to* [*Upon Breaking the Seal*] in 2004.

"the rain of the / meteor shower in Leo / lets up on the cancer ward": This poem represents what one might call a "translation game" in that Tada creates a poem that only takes on its fullest meaning when considered in relationship to English. As in one of the tanka translated in this volume, she plays with the double meaning of the English word "cancer." In the final portion of the Japanese original, she writes literally, "upon the crab constellation ward," aware that the poem will take on a special significance given that the crab constellation is called Cancer in English.

"so fresh / the pattern after sweeping / the summer sumō ring": Before and between sumō matches, sand and dirt is sprinkled over the clay surface of the ring in order to provide traction for the wrestlers' feet. Sweeping the ring between matches leaves the clean broom traces Tada describes in this poem.

"traces of you / grow still beneath / a myriad of green leaves": Tada met Yagawa Sumiko (1930–2002) when she was a college student and the two remained lifelong friends. Yagawa was a prominent translator, poet, and essayist, as well as the wife of the important avant-garde author and translator Shibusawa Tatsuhiko. The word *omokage* can mean "vestiges, traces" but can also refer to the way someone, especially their face, looks. Here, Tada seems to be sadly reflecting on the fact that her memories of Yagawa, perhaps her memories of her appearance, are slowly becoming still under the growth of a new season of life.

"the galingale— / my parents' home / so long after losing them": Galingale (*kayatsuri* or *Cyperus microiria* in Latin) is a kind of annual yellowish-green sedge that typically grows as a weed along roadsides, in rice paddies, and in other damp places. When left to its own devices, it can grow to between 12 and 20 inches high. This poem describes a garden where Tada's deceased parents once lived that is now, long after their death, choked with weeds.

"having completely forgotten / my head is light— / the rattan pillow": Because the midsummer months are often extremely humid in Japan, people sometimes use hollow flexible pillows made of woven rattan. These allow air to flow through and do not become damp with sweat.

"holding a jade cicada / how I want to listen to the cicadas / calling out like a summer shower": Cicadas create holes in the ground where they lay their eggs, which will incubate for as long as several years. Because the mature cicada emerges from these holes, the ancient Chinese came to see them as symbols of resurrection and would place jade cicadas in the mouths of the dead in the hopes of encouraging resurrection in the afterlife.

AFTER HALF A CENTURY

Tada refers in the second stanza of this poem to a legend of Krishna, who appeared to an ancient king of south India and challenged him to the game of chauturanga, saying that if he won, he would take the quantity of rice described in Tada's poem. By the time the king lost, he realized the quantity of rice he had to forfeit was greater than all of the rice in all the granaries of the kingdom.

TWICE ROUND THE LOOP LINE

Both Tokyo and Osaka have major train lines that form a loop around the center of the city and provide interurban transportation for countless millions of passengers each year. In the second part of the poem, Tada mentions Nippori, which is located on the northeastern part of the Yamanote loop line in Tokyo. The name literally means "village of the setting sun" (日暮里), which gives her the source of the word play in the first line: "Even if the sun is setting as I pass Nippori..." In Japan, there are numerous pilgrimage routes that involve traveling through an ordered series of temples or sacred spots. In this poem, Tada conceives of the Yamanote line, ridden by millions of people each day, as the same sort of meditative pilgrimage.

TURNING THE WHEEL OF TRANSMIGRATION

One of the treasures of the Hōryūji Temple in Nara Prefecture is the Tamamushi (Jade-Beetle) Shrine, created in the early seventh century. On one side of the shrine is an illustration of one of the Jataka stories (stories of the early incarnations of the man who would one day be reborn as the historical Buddha). In it, a young man sees a mother tiger with her starving cub. Feeling pity for her, he throws himself off a cliff to offer his body to them as food. This piece of art is sometimes called in English *The Bodhisattva's Sacrifice*.

GARDEN OF PARADISE

In the line that I have given the literal translation "Isn't this remarkably amusing?" Tada uses the word *ichijirushiku* (singularly, remarkably, strikingly), which sounds similar to the word *ichijiku,* meaning "fig"—the fruit that provides the main image for the poem.

SUMMER LETTER

As mentioned in the note to the poem "Yamanba," the word *utsusemi* means both "cicada shell" and, through metaphorical extension, "the body within this world." Likewise, the word *kami* can mean both "hair" and "god" or "gods." Although Tada uses the characters meaning "hair," the words she chooses are homophonic with another meaning, "As I let my mortal body settle with the gods." This poem was first published in 2002, after her diagnosis of cancer.

FROM *PERSON OF THE PLAYFUL STAR:* TANKA

This posthumous collection of tanka contains poems written over the course of the last few decades of Tada's life.

"for this last look / I've wrapped my body / in a thick gown and come / outside to meet the / clusters of falling stars": In 2001, there was a particularly dramatic meteor shower in the constellation of Leo that drew people across Japan onto their balconies and into their yards to watch. This was the same year Tada was diagnosed with uterine cancer.

"my diagnosis / of cancer was a notice / of pregnancy too / consecrated in the shrine of children / is the god of cancer": In Japanese, the word "uterus" (*shikyū*) is written with the two characters meaning "children" (子) and "shrine" (宮).

"my flesh / cut crosswise / to form round slices / tens of tomograms / lined up in a row": In this and subsequent poems, Tada compares the views of her body seen in tomograms to the kind of crosswise cut (*wagiri* in Japanese) used to slice radishes, carrots, logs, and other round items.

"if I were a tree / cutting me crosswise would / produce beautiful rings / but cutting my body just shows / an overgrown thicket": Tada uses the image of a thicket (*odoro*), which in classical Japanese verse is generally a place of confused, proliferating grassy growth, as a metaphor for the cancer proliferating in her body.

"accustomed to living / in a storehouse of grasses / I have seen / the leaves of language / flourish and wither away": The conceit of this point revolves around the literal meaning of the word *kotoba* (言葉), which is written with the two characters meaning "leaves" (葉) of "speech/language" (言) and which means "words," "expressions," or more generally "language." In classical Japan, the word I have rendered "storehouse" (*fu*) specifically meant a structure for storing written documents, especially official ones.

"face to face / with his beloved / the emperor has turned to stone / in a museum / in the old capital": As noted in the introduction, Tada translated Marguerite Yourcenar's novel *Mémoires d'Hadrien* [*Memoirs of Hadrian*], which focuses largely on the passionate love between the Roman emperor Hadrian and the beautiful young man Antinous. This and the subsequent handful of tanka were inspired by a trip that Tada made to Italy.

"what do they / intend to burn / piling these dessicated bones / high like firewood / as if to say *memento mori?*": Tada is probably referring to the Santa Maria della Concezione dei Cappuccini in Rome. Beneath the church is a crypt decorated lavishly with human bones.

"I who roll the dice / and play the game / am a person of the playful star / rolling through / the forbidden heavens": In this and the poem that follows, the words "playful star" are a literal rendering of the word *yūsei* (遊星), meaning "planet." Ancient astronomers saw the planets as "playful stars" that wandered across the heavens on their own idiosyncratic paths.

"the gods give birth to / people on this planet / a confused and wandering star / where heaven moves / and earth moves": Another word in Japanese for "planet" is *wakusei* (惑星), written with the two characters meaning "confused, lost, wandering" and "star." In this poem, Tada makes both the more straightforward and the idiomatic meanings of *wakusei* explicit, so this translation highlights both meanings.

Chronology

1930 Tada is born in Kita-kyūshū in southern Japan. She spends much of her youth in Tokyo but visits other places, such as her mother's hometown on the Aichi River in Shiga prefecture, during the holidays. During her youth and early adolescence, she reads incessantly, especially mythology, and studies *nō* theater.

1945 As bombing raids on the Japanese mainland intensify, Tada is evacuated from Tokyo to her mother's hometown. There she spends an idyllic half year far away from the war. Later in life, she calls this her stay in the "Peach Blossom Spring."

1948 Enters the Department of Foreign Languages at Tokyo Woman's Christian University, where she studies French literature. During her time there, she forms a lifelong friendship with Yagawa Sumiko, the young poet, translator, and future wife of the intellectual Shibusawa Tatsuhiko.

1951 Graduates from Tokyo Woman's Christian University and begins attending Keiō Gijuku University, where she again studies literature. Around this time she meets her future husband, Katō Nobuyuki.

1954 Becomes a member of the coterie magazine *Mitei* [*Undecided*], where she interacts with many avant-garde poets and writers.

1956 Publishes her first volume of poetry, *Hanabi* [*Fireworks*]. The same year, she marries Katō Nobuyuki and moves to Kobe, where they settle into a quiet house at the foot of Mt. Rokkō.

1959 Becomes a mother with the birth of her son Akira.

1960 Publishes the collection of poetry *Tōgijo* [*The Gladiator's Arena*].

1964 Publishes a Japanese translation of *Mémoires d'Hadrien* [*Memoirs of Hadrian*] by Marguerite Yourcenar, which receives tremendous praise in Japan. Over the subsequent three decades, she translates many other pieces of fiction by Yourcenar, as well as numerous works by Saint-John Perse, Claude Lévi-Strauss, Henri Bosco, Antonin Artaud, and other

French writers. Publishes the collection of poetry *Bara uchū* [*Universe of the Rose*], part of which was inspired by her experiments with LSD.

1966 Becomes a mother for the second time with the birth of her daughter Maya.

1968 Publishes the collection of poetry *Kagami no machi arui wa me no mori* [*The Town of Mirrors, or Forest of Eyes*], which describes mysterious, surreal cities reminiscent of those of Italo Calvino.

1970 Begins teaching French and European literary history and French language as a lecturer at Kobe College.

1971 Publishes the collection of poetry *Nise no nendai ki* [*A False Record of Ages*].

1972 The publisher Shichōsha collects her previously published poetry and publishes it in the series Gendai shi bunko [Modern Poetry Paperbacks].

1975 Publishes *Shimendō* [*The Four-Faced Path*], a collection of prose poems. Also publishes the collection of tanka *Suien* [*A Spray of Water*], which shows her skill at writing in the highly stylized language of classical verse.

1976 Becomes a regular contributor to and supporter of the coterie magazine *Kyōen* [*Symposium*] along with the poets Takahashi Mutsuo, Washisu Shigeo, and Aizawa Keizō.

1977 Publishes the book of essays *Kagami no teōria* [*Theoria of Mirrors*], which is recognized as an important work of cultural theory. Also publishes the book of essays *Koji no iraka* [*The Tile Roofs of Ancient Temples*].

1980 Publishes the collection *Hasu kuibito* [*Lotophagi*] and travels to Egypt and Kenya with her children. This is one of several trips that Tada made around the world in later years.

1981 Publishes the study *Tamashii no katachi ni tsuite* [*On the Shape of the Soul*] about the ways ancient thinkers conceived of the human spirit. Wins the Modern Poetry Women's Prize for *Hasu kuibito* [*Lotophagi*] and the Inoue Culture Prize for Arts and Letters.

1983 Publishes the collection *Kiryō* [*Spirit of the Season*].

1984 Publishes the book of essays *Hana no shinwagaku* [*Studies in the Mythology of Flowers*].

1986 Becomes poet-in-residence for a semester at Oakland University in Michigan, where she writes and assists in teaching a course in modern Japanese literature. Publishes the collection *Hafuribi* [*Ceremonial Fire*].

1987 Becomes instructor of French literature at Eichi University in Amagasaki. Later is given an appointment as instructor of religious studies in the university graduate school. Attends the World Writers Conference in Finland as one of two representatives for Japan (the other is Nakagami Kenji).

1989 Publishes two books of essays, *Kamigami no shimon* [*Fingerprints of the Gods*] and *Yume no shinwagaku* [*Studies in the Mythology of Dreams*].

1990 Katydid Books, published by Oakland University, releases *Moonstone Woman: Selected Poems and Prose* as part of its series Asian Poetry in Translation. The slim volume, which grew out of connections that Tada made while living in Michigan, contains translations of eighteen poems.

1994 The publisher Sunagoya Shobō publishes *Teihon Tada Chimako shishū* [*The Authoritative Edition of the Poetry of Tada Chimako*], which reprints all of her collections published thus far in a single volume.

1995 Wins the Kobe Municipal Cultural Prize for her contributions to local culture.

1997 Publishes the book of essays *Mori no sekai ya* [*The Old Man of the World of the Forest*].

1998 Publishes the collection *Kawa no hotori ni* [*Along the Riverbank*], which wins the Hanatsubaki Prize for Modern Poetry. Travels to Havana to participate in the International Cultural Exchange at the invitation of the Cuban Literary Association.

2000 Publishes the collection *Nagai kawa no aru kuni* [*The Land of the Long River*] about ancient Egyptian mythology and her travels in Egypt. Also publishes two books of essays, *Dōbutsu no uchūshi* [*A Record of the Universe of Animals*] and the autobiographical *Jū-go-sai no tōgenkyō* [*The Peach Blossom Spring at Age Fifteen*], as well as a book of puns and clever word games called *Jiyūjizai kotoba mekuri* [*Punning with Characters and Words*]. Goes to Rotterdam at the invitation of the Dutch government to participate in festivities held in conjunction with the four-hundredth anniversary of Japanese-Dutch relations. As a result of this visit, some of her work is translated into Dutch.

2001 Wins the Mediterranean Society Prize for her literature and the prestigious Yomiuri Literary Prize for *Nagai kawa no aru kuni* [*The Land of the Long River*]. Late in the year, Tada is diagnosed with uterine cancer. She opts not to have surgery and takes minimal medicine. Soon after her diagnosis, she retires from Eichi University.

2002 By spring, she has recovered to the extent that she goes to Kyoto with her husband to view the cherry blossoms. Later, doctors discover her cancer has metastasized and entered her bone marrow. By summer, cancer has invaded both legs. During the week, she stays under medical supervision, and on the weekend, she returns home to be with her husband and daughter Maya, who lives in the neighboring city of Ashiya. During this time, she writes a large number of haiku and tanka. Her book of essays *Inu-kakushi no niwa* [*The Garden that Spirited My Dog Away*] appears in print.

2003   Dies from cancer after a long hospitalization. At Tada's request, her close friend, the poet Takahashi Mutsuo, edits a collection of her haiku poetry, *Kaze no katami* [*A Souvenir of Wind*], and provides copies to all who attend the funeral. At the funeral, there is a reading of an original *nō* drama, *Otome yamanba* [*The Virginal Witch of the Mountains*], that Tada had published in the literary journal *Subaru* [*The Pleiades*] in 2002.

2004   Takahashi Mutsuo edits Tada's remaining free-form poems and has them published them as *Fū o kiru to* [*Upon Breaking the Seal*]. In this collection, Takahashi includes the haiku poems distributed at Tada's funeral.

2005   Takahashi Mutsuo edits a posthumous collection of Tada's tanka poetry and publishes it as *Yūsei no hito* [*Person of the Playful Star*].

Selected Works

All books published in Tokyo unless otherwise noted. Publications are listed in chronological order.

COLLECTIONS OF POETRY BY TADA CHIMAKO

Hanabi [*Fireworks*]. Shoshi Yuriika, 1956.
Tōgijo [*The Gladiator's Arena*]. Shoshi Yuriika, 1960.
Bara uchū [*Universe of the Rose*]. Shōshinsha, 1964.
Kagami no machi arui wa me no mori [*The Town of Mirrors, or Forest of Eyes*]. Shōshinsha, 1968.
Nise no nendai ki [*A False Record of Ages*]. Yamanashi Shiruku Sentā, 1971.
Tada Chimako shishū [*Poetry of Tada Chimako*]. Gendai shi bunko 50 [Modern Poetry Paperbacks 50]. Shichōsha, 1972.
Shimendō [*The Four-Faced Path*]. Shichōsha, 1975.
Suien: Tada Chimako kashū [*A Spray of Water: Tanka by Tada Chimako*]. Kobe: Kōbe Bukkusu, 1975.
Hasu kuibito [*Lotophagi*]. Shoshi Ringoya, 1980.
Kiryō [*Spirit of the Season*]. Chūsekisha, 1983.
Hafuribi [*Ceremonial Fire*]. Ozawa Shoten, 1986.
Teihon Tada Chimako shishū [*The Authoritative Edition of the Poetry of Tada Chimako*]. Sunagoya Shobō, 1994.
Kawa no hotori ni [*Along the Riverbank*]. Shoshi Yamada, 1998.
Nagai kawa no aru kuni [*The Land of the Long River*]. Shoshi Yamada, 2000.
Kaze no katami [*A Souvenir of Wind*]. Fukiage-chō, Saitama: Yūshin Bunko, 2003.
Fū o kiru to [*Upon Breaking the Seal*]. Shoshi Yamada, 2004.
Yūsei no hito: Tada Chimako kashū [*Person of the Playful Star: Tanka of Tada Chimako*]. Fukiage-chō, Saitama: Yūshin Bunko, 2005.

BOOKS OF ESSAYS BY TADA CHIMAKO

Kagami no teōria [*Theoria of Mirrors*]. Yamato Shobō, 1977. Revised edition, 1980. Reprinted Chikuma Shobō, 1993.

Koji no iraka [*The Tile Roofs of Ancient Temples*]. Kawade Shobō Shinsha, 1977.

Tamashii no katachi ni tsuite [*On the Shape of the Soul*]. Hakusuisha, 1981.

Hana no shinwagaku [*Studies in the Mythology of Flowers*]. Hakusuisha, 1984.

Kamigami no shimon [*Fingerprints of the Gods*]. Chikuma Shobō, 1989. Reprinted Heibonsha, 1984.

Yume no shinwagaku [*Studies in the Mythology of Dreams*]. Dai-san Bunmeisha, 1989.

Mori no sekai ya: Ki e no manazashi [*The Old Man of the World of the Forest: A View to the Trees*]. Kyoto: Jinbun Shoin, 1997.

Dōbutsu no uchūshi [*A Record of the Universe of Animals*]. Seidosha, 2000.

Jiyūjizai kotoba mekuri [*Punning with Characters and Words*]. Kawade Shobō Shinsha, 2000.

Jū-go-sai no tōgenkyō [*The Peach Blossom Spring at Age Fifteen*]. Kyoto: Jinbun Shoin, 2000.

Inu-kakushi no niwa [*The Garden that Spirited My Dog Away*]. Heibonsha, 2002.

MAJOR TRANSLATIONS BY TADA CHIMAKO

Many of these translations have been reprinted multiple times, but only the first publication is listed here.

Hadorianusu tei no kaisō [*Mémoires d'Hadrien*] by Marguerite Yourcenar. Hakusuisha, 1964.

San-Jon Perusu shishū [*Poésies de Saint-John Perse*] by Saint-John Perse. Shichōsha, 1967.

Revi-Sutorōsu to no taiwa [*Entretiens avec Claude Lévi-Strauss*] by Georges Charbonnier. Misuzu Shobō, 1970.

Zubon no robasuke [*L'âne Culotte*] by Henri Bosco. Gakushū Kenkyūsha, 1970.

Hariogabarusu: Mata wa taikan seru anākisuto [*Héliogabale, ou, L'anarchiste couronné*] by Antonin Artaud. Hakusuisha, 1977.

Kumo to tomodachi ni natta onna no ko no hanashi [*Histoire du nuage qui était l'ami d'une petite fille*] by Bertrand Ruillé. Kaiseisha, 1978.

Tōhō kitan [*Nouvelles orientales*] by Marguerite Yourcenar. Hakusuisha, 1980.

Raion [*Le lion*] by Joseph Kessel. Nihon Buritanika, 1981.

Hi [*Feux*] by Marguerite Yourcenar. Hakusuisha, 1983.

Tsumibito [*Le malfaiteur*] by Julien Green. Co-translated with Inoue Saburō. Kyoto: Jinbun Shoin, 1983.

Piranēji no kuoi nōzui [*Le cerveau noir de Piranese*] by Marguerite Yourcenar. Hakusuisha, 1985.
Shōnen jūjigun [*La croisade des enfants*] by Marcel Schwob. Ōkokusha, 1990.
Kono watashi, Kuraudiusu [*I, Claudius*] by Robert Graves. Co-translated with Arai Toshio. Misuzu Shobō, 2001.

ENGLISH TRANSLATIONS OF TADA CHIMAKO'S WORK

The Burning Heart: Women Poets of Japan. Ed. and trans. Kenneth Rexroth and Ikuko Atsumi. NY: Seabury Press, 1977 [contains one poem].
Modern Japanese Poetry. Trans. James Kirkup, ed. A. R. Davis. St. Lucia, Queensland: University of Queensland Press, 1978 [contains six poems].
A Play of Mirrors: Eight Major Poets of Modern Japan. Trans. Akai Toshio, Koriyama Naoshi, Edward Lueders, Kerstin Vidaeus, and Thomas Fitzsimmons. Rochester, MI: Katydid Books, 1987 [contains eight poems and an introduction to Tada's work by the poet Ōoka Makoto].
Moonstone Woman: Selected Poems and Prose. Trans. Robert Brady, Odagawa Kazuko, and Kerstin Vidaeus. Asian Poetry in Translation: Japan 11. Rochester, MI: Katydid Books, 1990 [contains eighteen poems].
Like Underground Water: The Poetry of Mid-Twentieth Century Japan. Trans. Naoshi Koriyama and Edward Lueders. Port Townsend, WA: Copper Canyon Press, 1995 [contains three poems].
"Winged Words: An Interview with Tada Chimako." Trans. Robert Brady and Akemi Wegmüller. *Kyoto Journal,* vol. 29 (1995).
Japanese Literature Today, vol. 24 (1999) [contains two poems translated by Adam Fulford].
The PIP Anthology of World Poetry of the Twentieth Century, vol. 4. Ed. Douglas Messerli. Los Angeles: Green Integer, 2003 [contains twelve poems translated by Hiroaki Sato].
Aufgabe, vol. 4 (2004) [contains one poem translated by Sawako Nakayasu].
Japan: A Traveler's Literary Companion. Ed. Jeffrey Angles and J. Thomas Rimer. Berkeley: Whereabouts Press, 2006 [contains one essay translated by Jeffrey Angles].
Japanese Women Poets: An Anthology. Ed. and trans. Hiroaki Sato. Armonk, NY: M. E. Sharpe, 2007 [contains translations of fourteen free-verse poems plus several tanka and haiku].

Credits

Several of the poems included in this book were first published in earlier versions in the following journals:

A few haiku from *A Souvenir of Wind* appeared in *Language for a New Century: Contemporary Poetry from the Middle East, Asia, and Beyond*, ed. Tina Chang, Nathalie Handal, and Ravi Shankar (New York: W. W. Norton, 2008), 148–49. Reproduced by permission of Tina Chang.

"From Dragon Teeth Sown in the Earth," "Labyrinth," "After Half a Century," and "The Piece of Mail, or My Nightmare" appeared in *Poetry Kanto* 23 (2007): 109–19. Reproduced by permission of Alan Botsford Saitoh.

A few tanka from *Person of the Playful Star* appeared in *Two Lines: World Writing in Translation* 14 (2007): 164–67. Reproduced by permission of Olivia Sears.

"From a Woman of a Distant Land" appeared in *Circumference: Poetry in Translation* 3 (Spring/Summer 2005): 8–13. Reproduced by permission of Jennifer Kronovet and Stefania Heim.

"The Town of Mirrors, or the Forest of Eyes" appeared in *Factorial* 3 (2004): 20–24. Reproduced by permission of Sawako Nakayasu.

"The Bodhisattva's Sea" appeared in *Buddhadharma: The Practitioner's Quarterly* 3.1 (Autumn 2004): 13. Reproduced by permission of the editorial staff.

"Shade" appeared in *Tricycle: The Buddhist Review* 14.1 (Autumn 2004): 128. Reproduced by permission of Anna Bernhard.

Index of Titles and First Lines

Poem titles appear in English followed by the original Japanese; first lines appear in italics. Prose poetry is indexed under the first sentence. Tanka and haiku are indexed under the first two and three lines respectively.

A child's eye   A green sprout shining with dew 17
A dark elephant from a dark forest 44
A firefly bobs up and down 77
a great iguana / dozing on the stone ruins 133
A high-pitched roar from the opposite direction 117
A letter will come from the day after tomorrow 119
A light is on in one corner of the nighttime garden. 54
A little while ago, a strange incident took place: a cat appeared out of nowhere and started running around my house as fast as a gale of wind. 55
a male mantis / quietly consumed 124
a person with a face / like in a 63
a short summer night / I wake as the flowers 124
a shower on / the taut nude form 128
A Single Lens [ひとつのレンズ] 15
A single rose— 28
a single trembling / of black hair 60
A summer of assertions 71
According to one theory, the kingdom never existed 66
accustomed to living / in a storehouse of grasses 131
Across the edge of a vermilion-dyed field 73
After Half a Century [半世紀が過ぎて] 114
after sixty years of walking / my shadow lies 127
Along the Riverbank [川のほとりに] 92
already reflecting / nothing of this world 125
although / the meaning is unclear 122
Ancient Love [古代の恋] 13
And then, the snow finally started to fall 23

As I thumb through the calendar 92
as the bandages are undone / I find myself / a springtime mummy 110
As the fruit upon the fig tree swells 118
as we move forward / rocked between 125
As we travel back upstream through the valley 98

because he spilled / the blood of tens of thousands 127
Behind a stone farmhouse 83
Boat [船] 107
born onto / this playful star 134
Boys of Summer [夏の少年] 70
Branching and converging, our paths cover the earth. 57
Breakfast Table [食卓] 17
Breeze [微風] 18
By the small entrance of the labyrinth (or the world) 78

Calendar in Verse [うたごよみ] 41
Carved around the tower of Vega 16
Ceremonial Fire [祝火] 81
Chewing on a Eucalyptus Leaf [ユーカリの葉を噛みながら] 101
Come out of the tunnel and 76
Contraction [収斂] 18
Cultivation [栽培] 116

Dark Sea [暗い海] 73
Darkness [闇] 28
Dawn (from *The Land of the Long River*) [曙] 108
Dawn (from *Fireworks*) [黎明] 13
dead souls— / the hydrangeas / lose their color so easily 112
Dead Sun [死んだ太陽] 27
Destiny of Paths [道のゆくえ] 57
did he give bread / even to the slaves? 132
dim evening light on / the base of my fingernails 60
dozing gently / with book in hand / the call of cicadas like a rain shower 113
drawing shadows / drawing gazes 129
dreams of travel or / perhaps travel in a dream 125
Dreams of Wearing Collars [首輪をはめた夢] 51

Entertainment [遊] 108
Epitaph [Epitaph] 15
even the gecko / by the window each morning / on such close terms! 111
Execution [死刑執行] 22

158   INDEX OF TITLES AND FIRST LINES

face to face / with his beloved 132
Facing the mirror, I put on my face 43
Fava Beans [そらまめ] 82
Finally after half a century, a clearly observable law has been found: 114
Firefly [蛍] 77
Fireworks in Morning [朝の花火] 22
Fish [魚] 116
Flow [流] 106
for this last look / I've wrapped my body 129
Fragments from Genesis [創世記残闕] 83
From a Woman of a Distant Land [遠い国の女から] 23
From Dragon Teeth Sown in the Earth [種播かれた龍の歯から] 93
From the Windows of a Journey [旅の窓から] 93

Garden of Absence [不在の庭] 54
Garden of Paradise [楽園] 118
Glaciers approach. The pain of their perpendicular lines! 19
Grammar of Summer [夏の文法] 71
Grave of Hyacinth [ヒヤシンスの墓] 40

having completely forgotten / my head is light— / the rattan pillow 113
he who made his way / into the forest 61
here too / in a remote region / I bend my knees and pick bracken 111
holding a jade cicada / how I want to listen to the cicadas / calling out like a summer shower 113
Horrors of the Kitchen [厨の怖れ] 74
How long has it been since I planted the eucalyptus tree? 101
how round / the fingers of the gecko / on the other side of the glass 111

I am on a train. 100
I am planted in the earth 17
I bathe / to my heart's content 130
I listen to songs / of someone handsome 123
I remember Pythagoras 82
I saw a lovely snake in a dream yesterday. 49
I stand someplace and watch 92
I travel through city streets where right turns are prohibited 91
I try to go back to my hometown / where wisteria hung 129
I turn back to look / and in my face / such wild abandon and pallor 112
I watch myself out of the corner of my eye as I get into bed and fall asleep. 51
I who roll the dice / and play the game 133
I who wait for myself 41

INDEX OF TITLES AND FIRST LINES 159

Ice Age [氷河期] 19
If I break the seal, something terrible will happen 115
if I were a tree / cutting me crosswise would 130
If you curl up and close your eyes 14
in the earth / countless corpses 128
in the grand hall / he made the strings quiver 123
In the midst of the crowd 18
in the morning breeze / the window of the wake room 126
in the pale light of / string music 61
In the pitch-black night sky 28
In this country, we do not bury the dead. 23
Inside the circular city walls is a town covered in water 31
It is Sunday, when the beheadings take place 21

karma of women / karma of men 127

Labyrinth [迷宮] 91
last night I was / a monarch in an 64
Legend of the Snow [雪の伝説] 23
Letter [字] 109
Like a loquat seed rolling over the tongue 18
Like a stake, the river penetrates 106
like a twisted rope / the karma of men and women 127
Like barley plants sending forth shoots 93
Lotophagi [蓮喰いびと] 66

May Morning [五月の朝] 17
may the water of / these short summer nights grow clear / the river of forgetfulness 112
Mirrors [鏡] 33
Moonstone Woman [月長石の女] 80
Moving 106
Murdered 107
My aunt who has descended from the mountains 116
my diagnosis / of cancer was a notice 130
my flesh / cut crosswise 130
my mother's arms / rolling up the reed blinds / were so white, so long ago 113
Myself [わたし] 17

Netherworld [冥] 107
Night Snow [夜の雪] 14
No matter how tranquil the home, there is always one room of foul portents. 74

of the nine holes of / the human body 128
Oh light! 15
Oh Odysseus, you who trained the wooden horse of pleasure! 38
old but still alive / father grows ill 126
On a sandy road lined with meager patches of grass 109
On earth where many bare feet have run 70
On the west bank live the dead 107
Once a year 108
once again / I follow the dark corridor 63
one cannot read / the rings of a tree in 131
one narcissus / draws close to another 60
One rosy morning 22

Peach Blossom Spring [桃源] 76
putting on a pair / of round clear glasses 63
Putting on My Face [化粧] 43

Rain washes away the remains of summer 18
Revisiting the Peach Blossom Spring [桃源再訪] 98
Right before the starving tiger who comes with cub in tow 117
River (from *The Land of the Long River*) [川] 106

Sea 72
Setting Sun [落日] 73
several volumes of / classical Chinese poetry 126
Shade [陰翳] 44
Sit properly, legs folded, before your tray 116
Slowly, slowly the man inhales 22
so fresh / the pattern after sweeping / the summer sumō ring 111
somewhere / in this crystal 62
Spilling twinkling droplets of light 27
Spinoza, each and every day for your daily bread 15
Start sliding, and you will not stop. 45
still leaning / the wooden marker 128
Stretching her supple body 108
Stretching their necks high 42
Summer Letter [夏の手紙] 119
summer passes— / the used book 121
Sunday [日曜日] 21
surrounded by my / thousands of tomes 123
swim on, old woman! / fallen cherry petals float / on the Milky Way 110

INDEX OF TITLES AND FIRST LINES 161

Tending to Plants [栽培] 92
That woman always sits in the garden 80
the Arab youth / speaks on and on 122
The biting wind of winter writhes. 19
The Bodhisattva's Sea [菩薩の海] 72
The break of dawn 15
The Cat of Momentary Extinction [刹那滅の猫] 55
the darkness of the snake / coiling himself up 61
the death / inside my body / is a soft winter wart 110
The divine ice has been smashed 40
The drifting sand on the desolate peak 15
the drowning victim / spreads her hair wide 124
the faint wind of the body / dislodges and blows 122
the galingale— / my parents' home / so long after losing them 112
the garden is / full of discarded cicada shells / full of holes 113
The Gladiator's Arena I [闘技場I] 20
The Gladiator's Arena II [闘技場II] 20
The Gladiator's Arena III [闘技場III] 21
The gladiator's arena slowly collapsed 20
the gods give birth to / people on this planet 134
the harshness of the / sound of the knife hitting 62
the holy child / is always at the breast 133
the hot water in / the abandoned kettle 62
The Housemate [同居人] 52
the linen clothes and Panama hat / my father had / so long ago 112
The Lost Kingdom [失われた王国] 66
The melancholic press together 20
The mirror is always slightly taller than I 33
The moonstone woman combs her hair 80
The morning breeze stirs the curtain 17
The Mysterious Woman of the Shadows, or The Valley of Sheep [玄牝あるいは羊の谷] 99
The observatory known as The Snail 93
The Odyssey, or On Absence [オデュッセイアあるいは不在について] 38
The old poet spoke of life 44
the palm of the hand / has both back and front 122
The palm trees circle round one another 13
The Piece of Mail, or My Nightmare [郵便物あるいは悪夢] 115
the rain of the / meteor shower in Leo / lets up on the cancer ward 110
the red of a / single autumn rose 65
The River (from *Along the Riverbank*) [川] 100
the round spoon / with the curvature 62
the slumbering / sky is purple 64

162   INDEX OF TITLES AND FIRST LINES

The snakes have all gone underground 98
the sun / over Mayan lands 133
The Territory of Children [子供の領分] 45
The town is nothing but mirrors 34
The Town of Absence [不在の町] 87
The Town of Mirrors, or Forest of Eyes [鏡の町あるいは眼の森] 34
The Town of Sleep [眠りの町] 31
the unaccompanied cello / illuminated in a small spotlight 123
the whereabouts of the wind / as it transfers / riding the grass 113
The Woman in the Garden [庭の女] 80
The Woman of the Thread [糸の女] 78
The world celebrates its beautiful weakness 81
the young leaves / all the shapes of hearts / the shapes of eyes 111
the youth flashes the / white soles of his feet 61
there are dead who / mingle with the north wind 126
there is a hole at / the end of night 124
there is a portent of / early death in those eyebrows 64
There used to be three of us in the house—me, my husband, and our young child who was hardly more than an infant—but recently, someone else seems to have moved in unannounced. 52
There was a time when I kept guard over a town of absence. 87
Thief of Fire [火の盗人] 83
This is the valley where sheep flow forth 99
This Island [この島] 14
This island is an island without wells 14
This night, this night only 73
though I climb / and climb 63
To a Retreating Figure [後姿に] 69
to the corner park / where I read my book 121
Tower of Vega [ヴェーガの尖塔] 16
traces of you / grow still beneath / a myriad of green leaves 112
transparent, the wind / passes through my palms held high 129
Tulips [チューリップ] 42
Turning the Wheel of Transmigration [輪廻] 117
Twice Round the Loop Line [環状線二曲] 117

Universe of the Rose [薔薇宇宙] 28
Upon the white face of darkness 83

Valley in Autumn [秋の谷] 98
various kinds / of wonders 131
Vestiges of Storm [嵐のあと] 15

Was it a sheep 13
Wayfarer [行人] 15
we place flowers upon / her pale, cold 125
what do they / intend to burn 132
when a cat in heat passes / the security light / switches on 110
Where many hearts were once stabbed 21
Why is only your retreating figure visible 69
will I die each night / and wander 64
Wind [風] 18
With flies that speak the language of men 77
with the fig leaf / he should cover his chest 132
Withered Field [枯野] 19
Within your breasts sleeps milk of marble 66
wondering / to what family 121

Yamanba [山姥] 77
yesterday, today, tomorrow / they are all a white field / in summer 111
Yesterday's Snake [きのうの蛇] 49

Text and display Garamond Premier Pro   *Compositor* BookMatters, Berkeley
Printer and binder Maple-Vail Book Manufacturing Group
■